RAISE YOUR VOICE

BY: JAIME VENDERA

The Incredible New Vocal System
Designed To Increase
The Range, Power, And Quality
Of Your Voice!

Copyright

The Voice Connection
Vendera Publishing

ISBN: 0-9749411-1-5
Cover Design & Inside Design: Molly Burnside
Photography: Molly Burnside, Diane Vendera
Artwork: Jason Burnside
Project Management: Stephanie Keen
Book Layout: Jaime Vendera

Copyright information for "Sky"
Words and music by
Sahaj Ticotin and Nandi Johannes
Copyright ©2002 Sahajamusic@ascap
& Rainchonwoogie@ascap
Published by Sahaj (ASCAP)

Quotes by Jim Gillette and Tony Harnell, used by permission.

RAISE YOUR VOICE

Since the original ebook release of **Raise Your Voice,** I have received hundreds of emails from around the world concerning my approach to vocal technique. The biggest issues have been centered on the fact that **the Voice Connection** is a rock vocals based website. If you are one of the singers who are wondering if the techniques in **Raise Your Voice** will work for all styles, ask no more! I present you with this simple answer; correct technique is correct technique! The techniques presented in this book are the most powerful tools I have found for strengthening the voice. This system will work for any style! If your goal is to become an amazing country vocalist, like **Wynona Judd** or **Vince Gill**, this technique will work for you! If your goal is to be the next **Luther Vandross**, or **Mariah Carey**…well, I can't make you sound like **Luther** or **Mariah**, but I can show you how to develop an amazing vocal instrument and present you with the tools needed for vocal success. If you want to be the next **American Idol**, I can give you the keys to unlock your voice potential. If all you want to do is be the vocalist in a **Soundgarden** or **Led Zeppelin** cover band, then I'll show you how to develop the strength and stamina to tackle songs by **Chris Cornell** and **Robert Plant**. No matter what you want to sing, the goal should be the same- to strengthen and develop the singing voice to your fullest potential.

Singers from all styles have studied with me; including pop, gospel, country, rock, hard rock, and of course, heavy metal. I consider myself more of a "voice-strengthening specialist. Although I spend a lot of time on style, with my students, my forte' is helping eliminate poor vocal habits and problems that most singers, including amateur, professional, and touring musicians, have to contend with. I teach singers how to strengthen their instrument and increase the range, power, stamina, and quality of their voices. This book contains the exact same principles that I teach to all of my students, including rock stars. Just remember, technique is technique, regardless of whether you are a beginner or a seasoned professional.

Every one wants a quick fix. There is no such thing. You are going to have to work for it. I've had new students come to me for one lesson and expect to walk away a superstar. It doesn't work that way. Anyone who tells you that they can dramatically transform your voice in one lesson is only in it for your money! Although I've seen amazing changes in singer's voices, it's all about the work!

Although there's no quick fix, I've decided to add a new chapter, entitled, **Advanced Techniques**, which contains some of the best tips, tricks, and tactics, for voice strengthening and improvement, that I have learned from professional rock singers, world renowned voice coaches, voice doctors, scientists, and my own personal experiences. I have also included over **80** new *Useful Tips* throughout the pages of this book, just for your benefit!

I have learned a lot since writing **Raise Your Voice**, and the conception of **The Voice Connection**. So, it's only right that I share my findings with my fans. I hope you enjoy this edition better than the first!

Good Luck and GOD Bless,

Jaime Vendera

THIS BOOK IS DEDICATED

TO THE MEMORY
OF MY GRANDPARENTS,

RON AND JEAN HADSELL

&

JIM GILLETTE

FOR
HELPING ME
TO FULFILL MY DREAMS

Special Note!

To access the audio files go to:
http://www.thevoiceconnection.com,
From the HOMEPAGE
Click on "Members Only"

The password is *"audiovoice"*

RAISE YOUR VOICE

Foreword

With your voice, you have the ability to form vivid pictures through sound...

You can produce intimate emotions, ranging from great joy to extreme sadness, all through the tonalities of your voice. Once you understand how it works, you will be able to apply your knowledge to strengthening the different aspects of your voice.

If you desire to improve your singing voice, and want to increase your vocal range, then you have found the right source. Although this is not a book of magic formulae for singers, it will give you the keys to unlock your singing potential. These keys have extended my upper range by more than an octave, in full voice, enabled me to sustain notes longer than I've ever imagined, and enabled me to sing as loud as 120 decibels. Applied properly, the knowledge contained in this book could extend your range, volume, and sustain time by much more. However, this range increase will not happen overnight. It will take hard work and dedication.

Trial and error best describes my case, and I mean a lot of it! I have been singing since I could talk, but I didn't start studying voice until 1988. Around that time, I was singing in a rock band, and doing fairly well, but I was having trouble hitting all the high notes with the same power and ease as all of my favorite rock stars. I listened to the popular rock singers of that time, and was awed by their vocal ranges. I just couldn't figure out how they sang so easily, especially night after night of touring. Singers like **David Coverdale** of **Whitesnake, Marq Torien** of the **BulletBoys, Jim Gillette** of **Nitro,** and **Tony Harnell** of **TNT** seemed to possess an uncanny natural ability to sing higher, louder, longer and stronger than any other singer on the planet, and I knew that they knew something I didn't.

Although I didn't have any of the answers, I kept singing songs too difficult for me; and the day after a gig, I could hardly speak as a result of the strain on my voice. I could always sound great that first night, belting out the songs and not worrying about the consequences.

Of Course, if we played the next night, I would struggle. I tried cheating by singing songs in falsetto instead of full voice, but **Guns-N-Roses, Led Zeppelin, Def Leppard** and **AC/DC** just didn't sound quite right when I sang these songs with a weak falsetto. Although this made it easier for me to sing night after night, my voice lacked the power and quality I had from belting out the tunes.

So I thought to myself, "What should I do?" Push myself to sound great and vocally suffer, or settle for the weak sound of my falsetto just to save my voice? I realized that I didn't have to settle for either choice. If other singers could sing with ease, then anyone should be able to attain the same results. Especially when several of my favorite singers had very deep voices when they spoke, but sang extremely high. I was determined to find an easier way, so I researched any available information that I could find about the voice.

I was obsessed with learning as much about voice as I possibly could. I took private lessons, dissected books, studied different styles and techniques, watched videos, and tried various vocal exercise routines. I even moved to Hollywood, California to study voice at the **Musician's Institute.**

Through years of experience and research, I have acquired an abundance of information about singing and the voice. There are multitudes of misconceptions about singing, and I've been through just about all of them. After over fifteen years of seriously studying the voice and figuring out what did and did not work for me, I decided to write down everything I could ever want to know about singing, in a journal. Although I originally intended this to be a journal for personal use only, positive feedback from singers and friends with whom I've shared my findings, finally convinced me that this journal was too important to be kept to myself.

I hope that you gain as much knowledge out of this book and program as I did creating it. To make it easier to read, I repeat certain principals and key words for your benefit. I assure you, this is not out of sheer laziness, but to make certain all the information I crammed into these few pages, commits to your memory.

If you follow the instructions in this book correctly, this program should help to save You all of the excess frustration, as well as the trial and error in time spent searching for ways to improve your singing voice. You can never learn too much about singing. I encourage you to continue to read and learn everything you can about the voice. I am constantly researching and studying the voice and I'll never stop! Hopefully this manual will become a major stepping-stone towards the improvement and self-discovery of your own sound. It takes a lot of hard work and dedication to **RAISE YOUR VOICE**, so good luck!!!!!

Part One   Understanding The Voice

It is important to understand the whole vocal mechanism before approaching the act of singing. If you develop a clear mental picture of what physically takes place when you are singing, it will make the vocal process easier. When you first learned how to drive a car, you had to understand the difference between gears like park, drive, and reverse, as well as how to steer. It was equally important to know the difference between the gas and brake pedals too. The same rules apply to the voice. You should learn what makes your voice run before taking it for a test drive.

Before taking your driver's test, you committed to memory certain traffic rules for safe driving. If you ever broke these rules, you could put yourself in danger. Singing follows along that same line, because several rules should be followed in order to protect your voice. These rules were created for a reason. If you break any of these rules, you could put yourself in harm's way, and your voice could crash.

The following chapters are broken into sections pertaining to different parts of the vocal mechanism. All parts ultimately work as a whole. When you establish a working knowledge of the voice you will better understand the vocal exercises found in **Chapters 17-19** of this book, making it easier to obtain the desired results at an accelerated rate. So, if you are ready to **Raise Your Voice**, let's move on…

RAISE YOUR VOICE

1 A Lesson In Breathing

Learning to breathe properly is one of the first crucial steps to singing. This is much like learning to crawl before walking. Let's begin by taking a long, deep breath. Breathe in slowly and visualize filling your entire body with air as if you were a balloon. Feel your lower abdomen expanding outward, all the way around your waist. Feel the sensation of your entire chest expanding until you are completely full. Next, steadily exhale until you feel that your lungs are completely empty.

This is considered one full cycle of breathing. In every day life you would not inhale as deeply and exhale as completely as you just did. This exercise demonstrates what an enormous lung capacity we possess. It also proves what little capacity we normally use. This deep breath is the energy we need to feed our singing voice; and what exactly are we breathing? **AIR**.

Have you ever blown on or waved your hand at a small wood fire? People usually do this to keep a fire going or from dying out. Why? Air feeds the fire. The flames will rise and the embers will burn brighter. For now, compare your voice to a bright burning flame. In essence, there is a fire inside of you. This fire, your voice, needs air to burn. When you release air in order to sing, you vibrate the vocal cords. You are adding fuel to the flames of your fire.

What would happen if you forced too much air on an actual fire? You could put the fire out. This can happen to your voice. Excessive air pressure from singing too loud forces bursts of air through the opening of the vocal cords (glottis). The vocal cords are delicate and should be treated with care. If this is the case with you, you will strain your voice by singing louder than necessary. Forced air pressure creates a loud and/or breathy tone, which rapidly dries out the vocal cords, leaving you with a dry, hoarse voice. Continuing such abusive vocal habits for extended periods of time can eventually cause you to lose your voice; you are putting out the flames to your fire, so to speak.

You must learn to breathe correctly, in order to gain maximum breath control. **Maximum breath control leads to maximum voice control**. Don't freak out and think that you must CONTROL your voice. This isn't the case. Singing should be a natural and relaxed act. What this basically means is that the way you breathe affects your singing voice. Air is your fuel. Air feeds the voice and provides the energy needed to sustain the song within you, but you must learn how to control the amount of fuel you feed your voice. If you do not breathe properly, your vocal cords will not vibrate properly.

There are three types of breathing that I am going to explain to you. They are **chest breathing**, **diaphragmatic breathing,** and what I like to call **maximum breath potential**:

CHEST BREATHING

Breathe in as quickly as you can, then hold it. What part of your body moved the most? I know I wasn't there, but I'll bet that your upper chest inflated like a balloon. Most people breathe entirely with their upper chest. This is the incorrect way for a singer to breathe and the way most people have learned to breathe. Chest breathing is limiting for a singer, only utilizing about one-third of your lung capacity. This limits your ability to sing long phrases; you won't have enough air to make it through the entire passage.

DIAPHRAGMATIC BREATHING

An improvement over chest breathing is diaphragmatic breathing. You might have heard it referred to as belly breathing because you allow your belly to expand as if you were breathing into the stomach. This type of breathing allows the bottom two- thirds of your lungs to fill with air, creating a larger air supply than chest breathing. More air enables you to sing longer phrases. The *diaphragm* is a muscle that controls the inhalation process. It rests above the stomach, right along the lower ribs, and divides the body in half. As you inhale, the diaphragm drops toward the abdominal area, creating room in the chest cavity for the lungs to expand. As the diaphragm drops, a vacuum is created within the lungs, drawing in more air. The stomach is forced down and out as the diaphragm muscle descends.

If the thought of a bloated stomach poses some concern, don't worry, because your stomach won't stick out enough to notice. I'd rather have my stomach stick out, than my throat blow out. If you are a practicing diaphragmatic breather, you are on the right track.

MAXIMUM BREATH POTENTIAL

Reaching your breathing potential is as easy as combining the two previous types of breathing to achieve your maximum lung capacity. This provides the best of both worlds. When you breathe with your chest, you are only filling the top one-third of your lungs. When you utilize diaphragmatic breathing, you only fill the bottom two-thirds of your lungs. When the lungs are full of air, they are similar to upside down triangles- larger at the bottom and smaller at the top. So, if you learn to fill the entire lungs from the bottom up, your breath supply will almost seem endless. Not every phrase you sing will require this much air. In fact, if you learn how to breathe correctly, you won't need hardly any air at all for singing. In time, you will learn to adjust the amount accordingly. Utilizing your **maximum breath potential** will allow you to grasp that extra lung space required for long phrases. You are probably thinking, "How should I apply this type of breathing to my singing?" Read on:

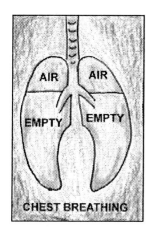

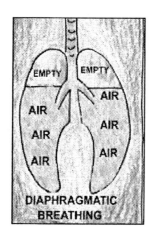

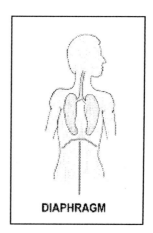

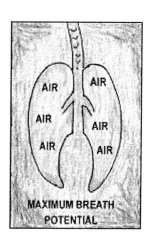

Useful Tip: The Truth About Maximum Breath Potential-
*What's the truth about **Maximum Breath Potential**? Although I explain to you about filling from the bottom up, and expanding all the way up through the chest, you don't actually need to take this deep of a breath during singing. But, the room is there if you'd ever need it. (Although it's doubtful you'll ever need this much breath.) The secret to singing is precise breath control with a minimal amount of air.*

LEARNING TO BREATHE AGAIN

Many voice teachers tell their students to sing from the diaphragm. This usually means that they want the singer to add more support to their tone by increasing breath pressure. It's rather difficult to sing from the diaphragm when it cannot support the tone and isn't actually used for increasing breath pressure. **Singing is an exhalation process. The diaphragm is mainly used for the inhalation process.** Your stomach and back muscles are used for exhalation, by forcing the diaphragm upwards, which releases air from the lungs. This is where your support comes from.

So, the "secret" to correct breathing is to **sing from your stomach, with concentration on the diaphragm**. You want to apply steady pressure with your stomach and back muscles, while visualizing breathing inward. I know this might sound a little confusing, so starting from the very beginning, let's go step by step:

The best way to learn how to breathe correctly is to lie on the floor with a book on your stomach. As you breathe in, "allow" the book to rise by breathing into your belly. This is the natural way to breathe. All babies breathe this way. Just watch a baby breathe sometime. Notice how their little bellies swell whenever they inhale. So you see, you were actually born with correct breathing habits, you just lost it along the way to adulthood.

When you have accomplished breathing on the floor, stand up and try expanding your stomach again. Did you happen to notice that your shoulders couldn't rise while you were lying on the floor? This is very important, because you want the shoulders to remain relaxed. Now, while standing, inhale and allow your stomach and sides to expand outwards. Breathing is a natural act; it should never be forced. **Do not allow your shoulders to rise.** If you do so, you are filling the upper one-third of your lungs first, which is essentially chest breathing. This mistake will prevent you from filling your lungs from the bottom up.

As your stomach expands, your sides and back muscles should expand as well. To make sure that your mid-section is fully expanding, put your hands in against your sides, thumbs pointing towards your back. As you breathe in, your hands should widen, fingers moving forwards, and thumbs moving backwards.

Useful Tip: Spread Your Ribs-

*To enable **Maximum Breath Potential** it is important that the very bottom ribs, or floating ribs (the small ribs at the bottom that are connected at the back to the spine, instead of to the sternum) expand out, to your sides. When using your hands to check for expansion, make sure that the floating ribs "push" your hands out. Try to keep the floating ribs expanded outwards as you sing, even when releasing your air supply.*

As your diaphragm drops, the lower organs expand downward and out in all directions, causing the bloated look. As you continue inhaling, the lower ribs (floating ribs) expand outward, making room for the middle to upper half of your lungs to fill up. The lungs should continue to expand all the way up your rib cage until the upper chest has slightly expanded.

Do not purposely expand the chest. Allow it to happen naturally. Concentrate on the feeling of the upper lungs expanding. There is absolutely no need to forcefully raise your chest; it will expand on its own. Remember not to raise the shoulders. If you do, you will create unnecessary muscular tension in your neck, which will cause your throat to tighten. With all of this accomplished, you are very close to your **maximum breath potential**, with the exception of one thing: **Correct posture**.

You must make absolutely sure that you try to observe correct posture. Poor posture limits full lung expansion, and creates tension throughout your entire body. To check your posture, stand up with your back against a wall, and your feet about a shoulder width apart. Your back should be straight. This aligns your spine, allowing the vertebrae to be stacked on top of each other in a straight line. When the spine is out of alignment, your body will be out of balance, and you will create unnecessary muscle tension. Walk away from the wall while maintaining the same position, and then wrap your hands around your neck. Stretch your neck, giving your head an elevated feeling.

If you force yourself to hold this position, you'll only end up distorting your posture. If you find yourself slouching, or forming any other distorting stance, re-check your posture. Allow yourself to physically feel the same as you did when you were against the wall **with your spine straight and your head elevated**.

Useful Tip: Stand Up Straight???

You are probably wondering, "Does this guy really expect me to stand up straight and sing completely stiff throughout the entire song?" No, not exactly. I have performed for years, and I know how demanding a singer's performance can be, especially in rock singing. I run around on the stage, crouch down, crawl on my knees, lean back when I sing high notes, and jump across tables. It's all part of the show. But, I try to re-establish my posture as much as possible to center myself and keep my body relaxed. Singing is all about physical freedom, and maintaining correct posture helps to inhibit muscle tension.

Now that you understand and have taken the perfect breath, what should you do with it? Do nothing at this point. You must first develop **breath control**. Without breath control there can be no voice control. To develop breath control, begin by taking a full breath of air and hissing it out in a steady stream. Consider a hissing sound to be a sustained "*sssss.*" Do not forcefully hiss the air out; keep the airflow as steady as possible. Did you feel the constant inward pressure in your stomach and back muscles? This is the physical sensation for which you are aiming when you sing. Your stomach and back muscles must stay firm...but flexible.

You should **NEVER** force the air out. If someone pushed on your stomach while you were singing, your stomach should go in very easily. **Never inwardly lock your stomach muscles or push your stomach out while singing.** Making your stomach muscles hard will tense the vocal cords. You are creating two problems; first, you are applying too much pressure by trying to force way too much air through (second) a now tightly clinched passageway. If you wish to physically feel this locked stomach position, try grunting. **Incorrectly locking your stomach muscles will lock up your vocal cords.** Allow the stomach to contract at its own natural pace.

Okay, I know that you just had a lot of information thrown at you, so let's try to make it a little easier. Breath control can be summed up in one paragraph:

When applying **maximum breath potential** to singing with a full breath and a slight tension in the stomach muscles, you must **always pretend that you are breathing in when you sing.** This is known as the *inhalation sensation*, and is the key to correct breath support. Just remember what it feels like to breathe in; your diaphragm drops, your stomach, sides, floating ribs, and chest expands. Concentrating on the **inhalation sensation** keeps the diaphragm from contracting as quickly and eases stomach muscle tension.

When the stomach muscles aren't as tight and the diaphragm doesn't contract as quick, you will be able to sing with less air pressure and less stress on the vocal cords. This is one of the keys to singing high notes. Most singers think that it takes a lot of air and loud volume to sing high, when just the opposite is the truth. Very little air is required, and if you use more air to increase the volume, you only increase the chance of hurting your throat.

So, before you begin to sing, take a deep breath through your nose, filling the lungs from the bottom up. Then, as you sing, **maintain a slight tension in your stomach muscles while you visualize that you are breathing in. Keep the floating ribs expanded out to your sides as long as you possibly can.** Keeping the ribs expanded works hand in hand with the **inhalation sensation**, helping to control breath release. You can put your hand on your sides to make sure your ribs remain expanded.

Still too much information? Well, let's simplify it even further:

1. **Take a deep belly breath in through your nose, (breathing in through the nose keeps the vocal cords moist), filling the lungs from the bottom up.**

2. **As you sing, maintain a constant steady pressure with your stomach and back muscles as if you were blowing out a candle, or sustaining an "sssss".**

3. **To counter-balance this pressure and minimize the airflow, pretend that you are breathing in (the inhalation sensation) while maintaining correct posture.**

Three easy steps should be simple enough. Mastering your breathing is a big part of the battle of mastering the voice. Correct breathing is both mental and physical. Practice this method of breathing until it has become second nature to you.

Useful Tip: Reach Up, Not Out-
*A typical habit that I catch students doing is stretching their torso upwards as they are inhaling, thinking that they are filling up the lungs correctly. No no, no. Keep the shoulders relaxed and breathe outward, all the way around your midsection. If you catch yourself reaching up, (sometimes, on the tips of your toes) STOP! This causes vocal tension and limits breath capacity. **Always breathe-out, never breathe-up!***

Useful Tip: An Extreme Breathing Exercise-

*Here is a great breathing exercise from my upcoming book, " **Mindset: Programming Your Mind (and Body) For Success**", that will help you to strengthen the lungs, diaphragm, and stomach muscles, while enhancing your metabolism through oxygenating the blood. Oxygen is such an important part of overall health. When the blood is rich in oxygen, your body will better fight infection and you'll speed up your metabolism, which will give you more energy and help you to lose weight... Because oxygen burns fat! This is why cardiovascular exercises are an important factor in calorie and fat burning. So, you see, you can improve your breathing for singing and get a little healthier at the same time!*

This exercise is really simple, but extremely effective. You must follow this formula in precisely the same order as it is presented. When performing this exercise, each count is approximately 1 second long:

1. *Inhale through the nose for 4 counts, and then exhale through the mouth for 4 counts. Perform this breathing step 5 times in a row.*
2. *Inhale through the nose for 2 counts, and then exhale through the mouth for 2 counts. Perform this breathing step 10 times in a row.*
3. *Inhale through the mouth for 1 count, and then exhale through the mouth for 1 count. Perform this breathing step 20 times in a row.*
4. *Pant like a dog, AT LEAST 40 times in a row, but you can pant for as long as you'd like. Then reverse the whole process for a warm down.*
5. *Inhale through the mouth for 1 count, and then exhale through the mouth for 1 count. Perform this breathing step 20 times in a row.*
6. *Inhale through the nose for 2 counts, and then exhale through the mouth for 2 counts. Perform this breathing step 10 times in a row.*
7. *Inhale through the nose for 4 counts, and then exhale through the mouth for 4 counts. Perform this breathing step 5 times in a row.*

*Are you getting a grasp of the equation? The count will ALWAYS be 4-2-1-PANT-1-2-4. If you decide to change the amount of repetitions that you perform a breathing step in a row, you must ALWAYS double the times for each step. Again, you can pant for as long as you like, as long as you at least double the amount from the last breathing step. So, if you decided to change the beginning count to 10, the new order would be like this: **10-20-40-80 pants-40-20-10.** I think you get the picture. In order for this exercise to be effective, you must complete the breathing sequence from beginning to end. If you feel dizzy, don't worry-it's just the sudden rush of oxygen to your brain. DO NOT DO THIS EXERCISE WHILE DRIVING! You don't want to be light headed behind the wheel of a vehicle!*

2 The Vocal Spark (AKA The Creation Of Tone)

Singing requires total mind-body coordination. To develop your voice to perfection, you must meet three requirements. **First**, you must acquire a basic understanding of the vocal mechanism. **Second**, you must project a clear visual picture in your mind of your perfect voice and the results you expect to achieve… And **third**, you must exercise the voice to meet the physical requirements of singing. All three requirements apply to every note in your range, from the lowest to the highest. All notes in your range should be equally easy to sing, although each individual note will have a different visual picture and muscular setup. With time, you will develop the muscular coordination and mental clarity needed to extend your range way beyond what you might have previously considered possible.

Let's begin by developing a basic understanding of the whole vocal mechanism. The vibration of the *vocal cords* produces all sound. The vocal cords are two thin membranes shaped like rubber bands, stretched across and housed in your *larynx*. The front part of the larynx is known as the Adams Apple. This is the protruding knot in the front of your throat. A woman's Adams Apple generally does not protrude like a man's, but it is still there. Put your hand on the front of your throat and swallow. Did you feel something move upwards? This is your larynx. Now yawn. This time, you should have felt the larynx move down.

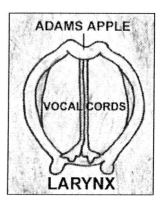

One purpose of the larynx is to close off the windpipe (trachea) when you are swallowing, to prevent foreign objects from entering your windpipe and lungs. Many times when attempting to sing higher, the larynx will rise high in the throat, much like swallowing, which closes off the sound of your voice. This closes off the upper trachea (pharynx), which is a main resonator. Voice training strengthens the vocal muscles so that you can control the position of the larynx without force.

The position of your larynx can vary, which affects the tone of your voice. When the larynx is high, the tone of your voice will sound nasal, as if you were singing or talking through your nose. Swallow to raise your larynx, and then hum. Did you notice how the tone sounds as if it were coming out of your nose? It sounds like you are speaking with your nose pinched shut. Next, yawn while saying *"ah."*

Did you notice the difference in tone between the two larynx positions? A low larynx position produces a deep tone like **Barney Rubble** from the **Flintstones** or **Yogi Bear**, while a high larynx position produces a thin, pinched tone like **Steve Urkel** from the sitcom **Family Matters, Fran Drescher** from **The Nanny,** or **Janice** from the sitcom **Friends**. If you force yourself to hold this position, you'll only end up distorting the tone and straining. **Larynx position example**

As you sing, you want to keep your larynx in a relaxed, neutral position. The normal position for the larynx when you are not vocalizing is balanced between a high and low larynx position. Once you learn to control your larynx through exercise, you can vary the position to change the tone of your voice.

As you breathe, the vocal cords remain open, allowing you to inhale and exhale without resistance. While singing or speaking, the vocal cords open and close at a variable rate (depending upon the pitch) as air flows between them. The vocal cords are trying to resist this air pressure by squeezing together, which causes them to vibrate. The raw sound of the vocal cords travels from the lungs, up the windpipe (trachea), and through the mouth.

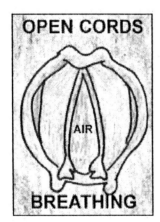 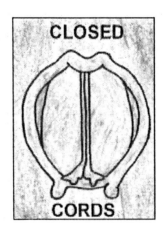 

At this point, the *articulators* manipulate the sound of your voice. Articulators are the physical aspects of a singer's body that help to form words and different tonal variations. The articulators are the teeth, tongue, jaws, hard and soft palate, and lips.

The *resonators* also affect the sound of your voice. Resonators are cavities in the body that emphasize *resonance*. Resonance is natural reverberation due to vocal cord vibration. This natural reverberation occurs when different areas of the body buzz with the sound of your voice. This is caused by the sound of your voice reflecting against bones. Your voice echoes and reverberates in the open cavities of the body, such as the chest, throat, and skull.

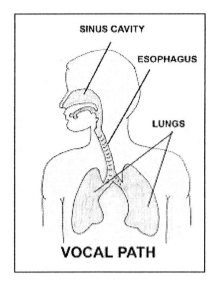

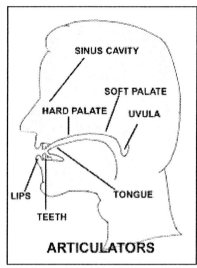

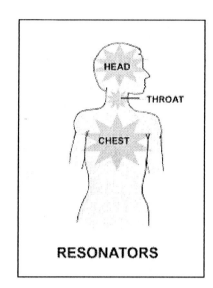

The main resonators are the chest, throat, and the head, although all parts of the body vibrate from the sound of the voice. The chest generally resonates in the lower portion of your range, the head cavity resonates in the higher part of your range, and the throat vibrates through your midrange. The majority of throat resonance is produced in the upper windpipe, above the larynx, which is known as the pharynx. As you sing from low to high, resonance travels from your chest upwards, overlapping into your throat, and finally into the head. When singing your highest notes, you will feel a strong buzzing sensation in the top of your head. It could even make you feel dizzy.

The buzzing sensation from resonance moves throughout the body depending on the *pitch* of your voice. Pitch is related to the range position of your voice and can be defined as how low or high the sound your vocal cords produce. This could be compared to pressing different keys on a piano. Each key represents a different pitch. Resonance produces several tones and pitches that are in harmony with the main pitch of your voice. This combination of tones and pitches is known as *harmonics*.

Harmonics are like little resonant echoes of the same pitch and harmonies of that pitch. The harmonics from resonance are not as loud as the pitch produced by your vocal cords, which creates a pleasant blend with the sound of your voice.

Useful Tip: Multiplying Echoes-
When you learn how to create multiple resonant echoes within your body, your voice will become richer, fuller, and louder, without straining your voice to accomplish this task. By practicing the exercises in this book, you'll learn to expand your resonance, thus creating multiple echoes, to create a fuller, more powerful sound.

You might be a little confused by the difference between tone and pitch. If **pitch refers to the range position of sound,** then **tone refers to the quality of that individual sound.** If you played the exact same note (or pitch) on a trumpet and a clarinet, they would produce the same pitch, but they would each have a different quality, or tone. The trumpet would have a loud bright tone while the clarinet would have a much softer, woody sounding tone.

The varying qualities are due to the different shapes and characteristics of each individual instrument. The same rules apply to singers. No two singers will have the exact same physical characteristics. If two singers were to sing the same pitch, you would hear two distinct tones. One singer might produce a deep, rich tone, while the other singer's tone is brighter and more vibrant.

Finally, the sound leaves your body and takes life. All parts of your voice are of equal importance. You must be equally balanced in breath control, vocal cord control, tonal control, resonation, and articulation… And these are just the physical aspects of singing.

To become a versatile singer, you need to develop your vocal style as well. However, style will only carry you so far. If you cannot control your voice, your range will be limited, thus limiting your vocal repertoire. One of the keys to vocal control is to understand what happens when your voice cracks uncontrollably and breaks in your upper range. It is important to learn ways to eliminate this problem. The so – called "vocal break" can be eliminated. The next few chapters will show you how.

Useful Tip: Mastering the Larynx-
A typical problem for beginning students is the "High Larynx" syndrome, on high notes. If this is a problem, don't sweat it for now. There are several keys to maintaining a neutral larynx position that you will learn in this book. By learning to maintain a "yawning sensation" when you sing and mastering an exercise, at the end of this book, called **The Bullfrog***, you'll conquer the "uncontrollable larynx.*

3 The Vocal Break

Imagine that you are singing a challenging song and you are approaching some difficult notes. You start sweating, wondering if you are going to be able to pull it off. You push with all of your might as you reach out for the highest note and – WOW - you hit it! But just when you think you've got this one in the bag, the veins in your neck start to bulge, your voice begins to waiver uncontrollably, and the next thing you know, your voice cracks, and you flip into a measly, embarrassing, weak falsetto.

That's a scary thought, isn't it? Every singer's nightmare is not being able to sing past the break point. For those of you who have had vocal training, I'm sure that the majority of teachers have said something like this: "You have reached your break point. It just isn't physically possible for your voice to go any higher, unless you sing in falsetto, and you will have to learn to deal with it." Although you must learn to deal with your break point, you do not have to be handicapped by it.

The break point is supposedly the point in your voice where you are unable to sing any higher, so you must learn to sing all notes above this point in falsetto. **THIS IS WRONG!** You have only one voice! Chest voice, mixed voice, head voice, falsetto, and whistle voice all originate from the exact same spot; your vocal cords. Although the sound might feel as if it is formed in different places throughout your body, it is only produced by the vocal cords. Your voice should be fluid and seamless. It should be one continuous, flawless instrument, throughout your entire range.

Look at an instrument analogy. A flute doesn't break on the way up the scale, nor does a piano. Neither should your voice. As with any instrument, the same principles apply to your voice. Tonalities and resonance of the voice change, but basic vocal principles stay very much the same. Lower pitches will produce a fuller sound, while higher pitches will produce a thinner sound. Each note in your range will have a different muscular tension and vocal cord positioning, but all of your notes are part of one single flowing instrument.

The vocal break has been widely preached about, but do not take everything you've heard as gospel. One of the best things you can do for yourself as a singer is to develop a true understanding of the so-called "vocal break." **The vocal break is simply a weak spot in your vocal range, along your vocal cords due to uncoordinated and untrained muscles. Your vocal cords are stretched to their limit at this point.**

When the pitch of your voice is low, your vocal cords are short and thick. As you ascend the scale, your vocal cords pull tighter, stretching from the back of your throat to the front, making them longer and thinner. You'll eventually reach a point where you cannot stretch the cords further without straining. At this point, your vocal cords are as long and thin as comfortably possible.

When your voice breaks, your vocal cords are trying to pull beyond this point. Pulling past this point will only cause your voice to crack and flip into falsetto, which would obviously cause the vocal cords to strain. Many vocal teachers classify singers by this "break point." Depending upon which pitch your voice begins to break you could be branded a bass, baritone, tenor, alto, or a soprano.

VOICE CLASSIFICATION

Vocal classification is simply a way to categorize the range of an individual singer, usually applying emphasis to the highest note of one's range. The following description will show the typical range and typical break point of each voice type. The number beside each note represents the pitch of the note relative to the notes on a piano. C4, or Middle C, represents the fourth C note on a piano. C5, or Tenor C, represents the fifth C note on a piano. C6, or Soprano C, represents the sixth C note on a piano. Each individual note is numbered by the octave it represents until the next octave is reached. For example:

C4, C#4, D4, D#4, E4, F4, F#4, G4, G#4, A4, A#4, B4, C5, …………….C6

CLASS	RANGE	BREAK POINT
BASS	*E2-E4*	*E3*
BARITONE	*B2-A4*	*E4*
TENOR	*D3-E5*	*E4*
ALTO	*A3-E5*	*A4*
SOPRANO	*C4-F6*	*E5*

These are basic classification guidelines. We could get very technical and discuss the falsetto range, multiple break points, vocal fry, and whistle register, or differences between Counter Tenor, Mezzo-Soprano, Coloratura-Soprano, etc., but these guidelines are all that you need for this book. I personally believe vocal classification to be unjust. This point of view can place serious mental limitations upon a singer.

RAISE YOUR VOICE

If you are to be put into a vocal class, you should be classified by your lowest note, not your highest, because it is easy to extend your upper range, but your lower range is dependent on the length and thickness of your vocal cords.

Your lowest notes are produced when the vocal cords are as short and thick as possible. A man's vocal cords are typically longer and thicker than a woman's, resulting in a lower speaking voice. This is due to the fact that the vibrating space (glottis) between the vocal cords is larger. The physical rule is that the smaller the vibrating space between the vocal cords, the higher the pitch. As far as high notes are concerned, the sky is the limit. Both men and women can sing Soprano notes in full voice, if they are willing to put in the time and effort that vocal training requires. Hopefully you won't let yourself get caught up in the vocal classification trap because as mentioned previously, your upper range can easily be extended through proper voice training and vocal exercises.

During my experiences in college, before I had began voice training, I was classified as a Bass/Baritone, because I could sing in the Bass range and my voice cracked on an E4 below Tenor C. I felt trapped, with no hope for change. For some time, I allowed vocal classification to put limitations on me as a singer. Now I just laugh it off, because I can sing many notes in the Soprano range as clear as a bell, as well as low Bass notes too. The next time someone talks about your "break point", just laugh it off and realize that the "break point" is not a limitation, but a minor hindrance that, as you will see in the next few chapters, can be overcome with patience, perseverance, and practice.

4 Understanding Falsetto

Falsetto is a term that is widely misunderstood. Basically, **falsetto is a light, breathy tone, with little resonance.** If you are wandering what falsetto sounds like, listen to the recordings of **Prince, King Diamond, Aaron Neville, Jeff Buckley, Justin Timberlake,** the **Bee Gees,** or **Justin Hawkins** of **The Darkness.**

Notice how the voices of these artists are thin and breathy on the higher pitches, with a feminine quality. I am not condemning the nature of their sound, nor am I stating there is anything wrong with singing in falsetto. All of these singers have incredible voices, and they have sold millions of records singing this way!

A lot of people use falsetto for their upper range because they are not capable of singing any higher in full voice. It is generally easier to sing in falsetto than in full voice. I have even heard one of the previously mentioned artists actually say that they sing everything in falsetto because it hurts their throat too much to sing in full voice. It is okay to use falsetto, as long as you are not using it as your last resort. You will become a better singer if you learn to use your full voice for the extent of your range, and if you desire, interweave falsetto throughout your songs for color and emotion.

THE FALSETTO MYTH

It has been falsely taught that a man reaches a certain area of his voice at which point he cannot physically sing any higher. This point is referred to as the **vocal break.** To sing beyond the vocal break, the singer must switch his voice into falsetto, in order to prevent the voice from cracking, thus enabling the singer to ascend higher up the scale. There is no truth to this. This is just a feeble attempt by some vocal instructors and singers to avoid their break point. **Any note that you are able to sing in falsetto, you can learn to sing just as easily in full voice.** In fact, you can extend your full voice higher than your falsetto if you are willing to put in the practice time.

HOW IS FALSETTO PRODUCED?

Let's start off with how falsetto is not produced. I was originally taught that falsetto occurred when two membranes that reside above the vocal cords, referred to as the false vocal folds, vibrate together. The false folds supposedly vibrate without touching, while the true vocal cords remain still. In order for a vocal vibration to occur, the cords must touch and release as air flows between them at a constant rate. Due to the fact that the false folds never touch, they cannot possibly vibrate, therefore they cannot produce sound.

All sounds are produced by the vocal cords, including falsetto! While full voice is produced when the vocal cords retain a consistent tension, falsetto is produced when there is not enough tension in the muscles that pull and squeeze the vocal cords together. When this occurs, the vocal cords vibrate loosely, allowing more air to escape, thus producing a breathy tone. **So much air is allowed to escape between the cords that very little area of the vocal cords actually vibrate.**

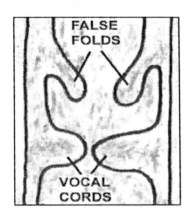
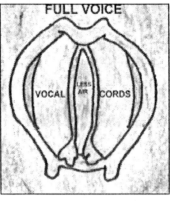
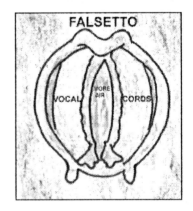

| **ONLY CORDS VIBRATE** | **FULL VOICE=LESS AIR AND FIRM CORDS** | **FALSETTO=MORE AIR AND LOOSE CORDS** |

Again I repeat **falsetto is simply a weak, breathy tone, with little resonance.** Remember the following statement and you will never forget the difference between full voice and falsetto:

LOOSE VOCAL CORDS = FALSETTO

FIRM VOCAL CORDS = FULL VOICE

Do not discount the value of falsetto; it is one of the greatest tools you could ever possess for developing your singing voice to its fullest potential. You will soon learn that falsetto is the basis for developing, strengthening, and increasing the range of your full voice.

5 The Zipper Technique

As you ascend the scale, the vocal cords pull tighter and become thinner, elongating themselves until they can pull no more. At this point, the vocal cords can do one of two things:

1.   They can try to pull tighter, only causing your voice to break and flip into falsetto, or,

2.   They can squeeze together from the back of the throat to the front, causing the pitch to rise.

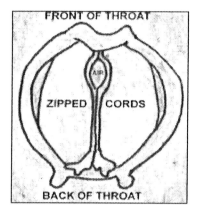

Squeezing from the back of your throat to the front is much like zipping a zipper. The squeezing makes the vibrating space (glottis) in the front of the vocal cords smaller. The technical term for the zipping of the vocal cords is **adduction**. It has also been referred to as **damping** or **dampening**. By narrowing and shortening the vibrating space, you raise the pitch. **A smaller vibrating space will result in a higher pitch.**

The **zipper technique** is performed in tiny increments along the edge of your vocal cords. With each individual increment a different pitch is produced. The throat and neck muscles help to do the zipping, and if done correctly, higher pitches are effortless. Remember, a higher note does not require any more air pressure or volume than a low note, just a great deal of practice to coordinate the vocal muscles.

An easier way to understand the **zipper technique** is by performing the **rubber band experiment**. All you need is two sets of hands and two different size rubber bands. Start by separating the smaller, thinner rubber band with your fingers. The thin rubber band refers to the size of a female's vocal cords, while the thick rubber band refers to a male's vocal cords.

Spread your fingers wide enough to produce tension in the rubber band. Next, have your partner strum the rubber band with their finger. The rubber band will produce a low pitch. The vocal cords are thick and pulled to a slight tension. Continue to stretch the rubber band apart. You will notice that the pitch rises as the rubber band gets longer and thinner.

Stretching the rubber band is very similar to the stretching of the vocal cords. The higher you sing, the longer and thinner the vocal cords become. There will come a point when you shouldn't stretch the rubber band any further. Stretching beyond this point will cause the rubber band to snap. You have just reached your break point.

Since you can't actually see the vocal cords stretching, you must rely on feeling. If you start straining or your voice breaks, then you know that you are stretching your cords too far, and beyond your natural break point.

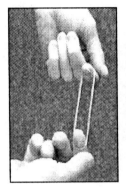    

CHEST   BEFORE BREAK   AT BREAK   THROAT   HEAD

When you have reached the safe extent of stretching the rubber band, have your partner squeeze one end of the rubber band together while strumming the other end. The pitch rises and is easier to produce. You have just shortened the vibrating space to obtain higher pitches without stretching the rubber band beyond its stress point. This illustrates the **zipper technique** that must be applied to your own voice. The higher you slide your fingers, decreasing the vibrating space, the higher you raise the pitch. **The vocal cords zip together tighter and tighter, continually shortening the vibrating space, thus raising the pitch!**

This experiment is a valuable tool for understanding the pitch process of the vocal cords. When you complete this experiment, repeat again with the thicker rubber band. You will notice that the beginning pitch is much lower than the first time you performed the experiment. As I previously stated, the smaller, thinner rubber band emulates a female's voice, while the longer, thicker rubber band mimics a male's vocal cords.

Before we move on, lets refer back to pictures 1-5 again. It's very important that you grasp the concept of the cords zipping together, and understand exactly when and where this is taking place in your own voice. Picture 1 demonstrates your voice at your lowest pitch, which is called chest voice. As you ascend the scale, the vocal cords become longer and thinner. Picture 2 shows a tighter pull, but you are still singing in chest voice. When you reach the point where your voice begins to break or you begin to strain, the vocal cords must begin to zip together, as in picture 3. This pitch is typically around E4, above Middle C for males, and A#4, below Tenor C for females.

The area right above the break (picture 4) is the area of throat resonance, (pharyngeal resonance) or your middle voice, and typically lasts for about 5-7 notes before you reach head resonance, or head voice. Picture 5 shows the cords zipping together very tightly. The pitch is very high at this point and the sound produced by the vocal cords will be in head voice. Head voice, or head resonance usually begins around an A4-B4 below Tenor C for males, and a D5-E5 above Tenor C for females. Resonance, chest voice, mid-voice, and head voice will be explained shortly.

Useful Tip: What's the "Whistle Voice?"

*Have you ever heard of "whistle voice"? This is a high pitch above the soprano range that sounds like the vocal cords are "whistling". This register was made very popular by singers like **Mariah Carey** and **Adam Lopez**. In fact, **Adam** beat out **Mariah** to become the **Guinness World Record** holder for the highest note. These pitches are attained when the cords "zip up" even tighter than head voice notes. The cords will squeeze together so tightly at the front of the throat, that the glottis will become almost as small as a pinhole.*

RESONANCE PLACEMENT

Understanding the **zipper technique** is an important part of developing your voice to its fullest potential. Since you cannot actually see the vocal cords as they zip, you need a way to identify with the sensations of your vocal cords when zipping takes place. If you focus on your vocal cords, you can actually feel the cords zipping together. This is challenging. It's much easier to trust the sensation of resonance in your body than to trust the physical sensations of the muscles in your throat. *Resonance placement* is an easier way to identify the zipping of the vocal cords.

What is resonance placement? Resonance placement simply refers to following the path of resonance within your body. Put your hand flat against your chest and hum a low note. Can you feel your hand vibrating from the buzzing sensation in your chest? This is chest resonance. As you sing up a scale, the resonance (buzzing sensation) will travel from deep inside of your chest to high in the top of your head. Hum on a higher note with your mouth closed. Could you feel your head and teeth buzz? This is head resonance.

The best way to utilize resonance placement, as applied to the **zipper technique**, is to imagine a ping-pong ball floating on a steady stream of air, within your physical body, much like the floating balls balanced in tall clear cylinders for televised lottery drawings. Imagine a tall clear cylinder within your body rising from the center of your diaphragm, straight up through your body to the very top of your head. The ping-pong ball floating inside of this cylinder is your *core of resonance*.

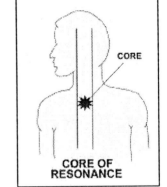

The **core of resonance** is your central point of vibration, or the core of the buzzing sensation. Although your resonant focal point is upon this imaginary ping-pong ball, resonance radiates out much farther, more like the sun radiating outwards, resonating every single cell of your body.

When you are vocalizing on low pitches, visualize your **core of resonance** balanced down in your chest, sitting right on top of your diaphragm. When singing high pitches, visualize your **core of resonance** floating in your head. As you sing from low to high, your **core of resonance** rises from low to high. The most intense point of resonance should be balanced upon the core. If you imagine your **core of resonance** radiating outwards, you'll create stronger resonant (buzzing) vibrations, making it easier to zip without straining your voice. **The stronger the buzzing sensation, the easier the cords zip together.**

Both the **inhalation sensation** and the **core of resonance** visualizations help to improve your breath support, by developing the balance of pressure between your diaphragm, and your stomach muscles. **The more resonance produced, the less breath pressure required.** Less breath pressure means less stress on the vocal cords. One of the main reasons singers lose their voice is because they apply too much breath pressure.

Singers tend to think that they must sing louder in order to sing higher. This is a fallacy. By focusing on resonance and the **inhalation sensation,** you'll minimize breath pressure and help eliminate this problem.

When you start to feel the resonance rise up out of your chest and into your throat, your vocal cords should be pulled as tightly as they can possibly stretch, without straining. At this point, your cords start zipping together. They continue to zip together in tiny increments from the back of the throat to the front, as the resonance rises upward from your throat, right above the vocal cords (pharynx) and into your head. When you feel the buzzing sensation in your head, you can be sure that your vocal cords are zipping together correctly, and you shouldn't be straining.

IDENTIFYING YOUR CORE OF RESONANCE

If you are having trouble following your **core of resonance,** use the following as a guideline:

When following your **core of resonance,** your lowest note will rest right on top of the diaphragm. The **core of resonance** will continue to rise up in the chest until your voice breaks or cracks. This is a sign that it is time for the cords to start zipping together. The entire area below your break point is called **chest voice.** At your break point, the **core of resonance** is right in the indenture of the collarbone, ready to rise into the throat. Remember, the break point is typically E4 for males and A#4 for females. The **core of resonance** will continue to rise up the throat, through the pharynx, for five to seven notes. These notes will be produced in the throat. Some coaches refer to this area as **middle voice,** or, a mix between the registers. I simply view it as a thinning of the tone as you ascend the scale. By the sixth, seventh, or eighth note, you should begin to feel the **core of resonance** pushing up on the soft palate in the back of your throat. You are now moving into head resonance, or **head voice.** The cords are zipping together in very tiny increments, so while in head resonance, the **core of resonance** should rise in very tiny increments. You could very well have more than an octave in head resonance to cover from about eye level to the top of the head. Head resonance is an amazing thing, filling your entire skull with multiple echoes, like a tiny cathedral. Sometimes it is difficult to pinpoint the exact location of your **core of resonance** while singing high, so, **concentration** is a must!

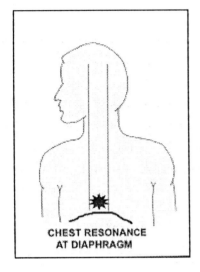
CHEST RESONANCE
AT DIAPHRAGM

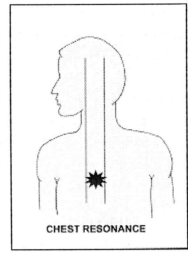
CHEST RESONANCE

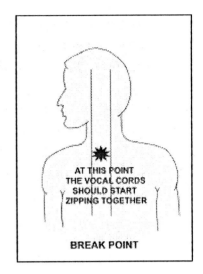
AT THIS POINT
THE VOCAL CORDS
SHOULD START
ZIPPING TOGETHER

BREAK POINT

If you start feeling dizzy on the high notes, don't worry, you won't pass out. Like I said, you've got a tiny cathedral in your head. Dizziness is a good thing and is due to the new sensations of head resonance. This is proof of proper **zipper technique** and plenty of resonance. As I previously mentioned, the stronger the buzzing sensation you create in your head, the easier your cords will zip together. So if you radiate your core and concentrate on the buzzing sensation, the higher notes will come easily. **THIS VISUALIZATION IS THE MAIN KEY TO LEARNING HOW TO SING HIGH NOTES IN FULL VOICE, SO WORK HARD!!!** Happy zipping!!!

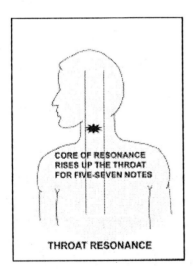
CORE OF RESONANCE
RISES UP THE THROAT
FOR FIVE-SEVEN NOTES

THROAT RESONANCE

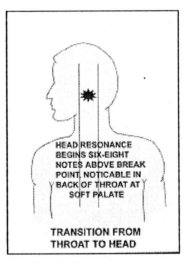
HEAD RESONANCE
BEGINS SIX-EIGHT
NOTES ABOVE BREAK
POINT, NOTICABLE IN
BACK OF THROAT AT
SOFT PALATE

TRANSITION FROM
THROAT TO HEAD

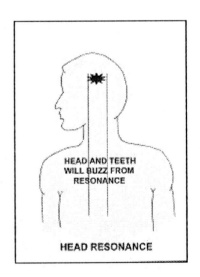
HEAD AND TEETH
WILL BUZZ FROM
RESONANCE

HEAD RESONANCE

Useful Tip: The Triangle-

When trying to get the cords to zip, it has always helped me to visualize the voice in the shape of a triangle- wide at the bottom of your range, (like the base of a triangle), and thin and pointy at the top of your range, like the tip of a triangle. As you ascend the scale and your cords begin to zip, imagine your voice thinning and aiming more towards a point, just like the sides of a triangle coming closer and closer together while aiming towards the top. It also helps to think "less baggage" as you ascend the scale. You don't need all of that pressure and fullness (vocal weight) that you feel at the bottom end of the scale, so don't push the sound up, let it float up the sides of the triangle and thin out. (This coincides with the **Core of Resonance** *rising as the voice thins.) When I mentioned this to* **Tony Harnell***, he totally agreed.*

Useful Tip: Some Don'ts of Cord Zipping!

You should NEVER clench your throat or grunt, for a louder sound, or to get the vocal cords to zip together! Only by practicing the visualizations and exercises in this book, will you be able to create the muscular coordination and muscle memory required to do the trick. As hard as it may seem, you must separate your mind from your throat. The cords are very small. They are approximately ½" in females, and between ¾"- 1" in males. You should never tense the throat area and jeopardize the health of these precious, tiny music makers. So, change your thinking about what it takes to sing high and go with the flow!

Useful Tip: The Power Push-

There is a "secret" way to tighten the stomach muscles to make it easier to reach high notes (get the cords to zip), and to achieve more power and volume, if this is what you require. I call this technique the **Power Push***, and I'll be explaining it in detail at the end of the book. For now, all you need to know is that there is ONLY one correct way to tighten the stomach. The "secret" is to push and tighten straight down towards the ground. This is the same feeling you get when you sneeze, cough, or go to the bathroom.*

Useful Tip: The Kazoo-

Have you ever played a kazoo? This funny little instrument is perfect for demonstrating the buzzing sensation you want to feel on your teeth. There is a small piece of wax paper in a kazoo that vibrates from your breath. Purchase a kazoo and hum a few tunes into it, then assimilate that same buzzing sensation against your teeth. (You'll also feel it in your mouth and sinuses.) Notice how the small piece of wax paper buzzes like a bee or a fly. This is the same buzzing sensation that you should aim for when you sing and is most noticeable by humming.

6 Hydrating The Voice

Water is the liquid of a singer's soul. It is one of many essentials for a healthy voice, and a healthy body. It is water that does the body good. If we compare our bodies to an automobile, then water is our oil. It is an absolute must for anyone with a serious devotion to improving the voice. Without water, the sound of your voice will lack the beautiful quality all singers strive for.

With the demands of singing, one must keep one's voice well lubricated at all times. The vocal cords must be constantly lubricated to maintain their elasticity. **Only water can provide this lubrication**, not soda, tea, coffee, or alcohol: only **plain, fresh water will work**. Natural juices help to hydrate the voice, and are an excellent source of vitamins and minerals. But, the body considers juice a food to be digested, taking a considerably longer time to hydrate the voice.

Water is the only liquid that is not processed as a food. When you drink water, it is not digested. It passes directly into your bloodstream and is distributed throughout the entire body, concentrating on the places it is most needed. It takes approximately twenty minutes before your vocal cords receive any hydration from a drink of water. Even after the cords receive lubrication, the water can evaporate quickly if you are singing.

If you are doing a lot of singing, the air pressure between the cords can quickly dry them out, especially from singing in a typical falsetto. So what do you do? You drink lots and lots of water. First thing in the morning, drink water, with meals, drink water, at night before bed; **drink water**. I can't say it enough. **DRINK WATER!!!** If you consume alcohol or caffeine products, be aware that **caffeine is a diuretic and alcohol is a dehydrator; they are both going to dry out your throat**. I'm not telling you that you have to give up your vices. I was the world's worst caffeine junky. Just make sure that you drink plenty of water to counteract dehydration.

I drink approximately a gallon of water a day. I know that's a lot, but I used to drink more. A good rule of thumb is half an ounce of water per every pound of body weight per day. If you weighed 150 pounds, you should drink at least 75 ounces of water a day, if not more. I know that sounds like a lot, but that's actually less than four, 20-ounce bottles of pop. (I weigh around 180 pounds, but I really like my water). So check your weight and adjust accordingly.

RAISE YOUR VOICE

Tony Harnell, lead singer of the rock group **TNT**, couldn't emphasize enough to me about the importance of drinking water. Here's what he had to say about the importance of drinking water:

"What you're really trying to do is moisturize the voice; as much moisture as possible. I recommend more than anything, drinking tons of water, and I mean from the time you wake up until the show at night. You will pee a lot, but who cares. The more hydrated you are, the better. Someone once said to me, "clear pee- clear voice." That makes sense."

This doesn't mean to drink it all at once. You have all day, so spread it out. I usually wake up and drink a 20-ounce bottle of water to get my day started, and then I sip on a bottle of water throughout the entire day. I drink water with all of my meals, even if I drink pop. Water aids the stomach with the digestion process. I always drink at least 8-10 ounces of water before I go to bed. I know this means more nighttime trips to the bathroom, but your body will thank you for it. You may also want to purchase a warm air humidifier for your room. This will humidify the air and help keep your voice moisturized while you sleep. Water aids the elimination process; helping to flush the kidneys, thus flushing out more toxins, so don't be surprised if you generally feel better.

While singing or exercising, you should drink water at room temperature. Drinking cold water or ice water can shock the vocal cords, causing the vocal cords to contract. Working out your voice is like working out on a treadmill. When your muscles are warmed up, your heart is pumping, and your body temperature is rising. If someone threw cold water on you while you were working on the treadmill, your whole body would tense up. The same is true with the vocal cords; it's just not as noticeable. Cold water prevents the vocal cords from zipping properly, thus shrinking your range. Room temperature water keeps the cords pliable, aiding the zipping process.

Now (on the next page) I'd like to mention several ways to hydrate the voice; you can **breathe in through your nose, breathe steam, inhale mist**, or **gargle water**:

BREATHE IN THROUGH YOUR NOSE

Although it might not seem that important, breathing in through your nose will make a difference when it comes to keeping the vocal cords moist. When you breathe in through your mouth, you are basically breathing in dry air. The sinus passages moisten the air before it is inhaled into the lungs, which will help to prevent from drying out the vocal cords. So, if possible, **breathe in through your nose when you sing!** I know this isn't always possible, or probable, but I personally recommend it. Not only will this moisten the vocal cords, but also breathing this way will assure that you breathe correctly, filling your lungs from the bottom up.

*Some singers and teachers, such as **Tony Harnell** do not follow this philosophy. Certain teaching methods focus on using and open mouth only, for breathing while singing. If mouth breathing works for you, that is fine. Singers such as **Jim Gillette** and myself prefer to breathe in through our nose. Do what works best for you.*

BREATHING STEAM

Don't you just love to sing in the shower? I do. When you're singing in the shower, it seems as if you have no limits as a vocalist. You feel like a vocal god. This feeling of vocal immortality is the result of three aspects:

1. There's no one watching you, so you'll generally feel less nervous. If you aren't dealing with your nerves, you will be relaxed, and you will sing more openly.

2. The walls of a shower will reflect the vocal vibrations, causing an echo. This natural reverberation makes your voice sound fuller, and sweeter.

3. **STEAM!**

Breathing steam does many things for your voice. The warm mist moisturizes and warms the vocal cords. It helps to open up the lungs and clogged sinuses. This loosens phlegm in the lungs, sinuses, and on the vocal cords. Congestion can affect your breath control, pinch off your sound, and worst, keep the vocal cords from vibrating properly.

Breathing steam is a great tool for anyone to use, especially before a gig. However, you can't always take a shower right before you go on stage. So what do you do? You could purchase a little portable electric steamer. You just plug it in, add a little water, and inhale. It works great! Not only does breathing steam help to open you up, but it also warms the vocal cords and relaxes all the muscles involved with singing. It's just like taking a steam bath, which relaxes your whole body.

USEFUL TIP: Quick Steaming-
If you don't want to carry around a portable steamer, you can breathe steam from a hot water faucet. Cover your head with a towel and bend over the faucet, draping the towel over the sides of the sink. This will trap the majority of the steam inside the towel while you breathe. It is important to hydrate the vocal cords as much as possible.

To keep your cords healthy, you should steam before and after a vocal performance. During a performance, your vocal cords get really pumped up. They need a chance to return to normal after the performance is over. This is just like jogging; you must slow down to a walk instead of stopping mid-stride. Immediately stopping from an intense jog will cause the muscles to tighten and tense up. Like your muscles, your cords are swollen, and need to slowly return to normal.

So, how do you keep your voice hydrated during your performance? One way is to always keep a bottle of drinking water with you on stage. But water will still take approximately twenty minutes to reach your vocal cords. If only there was a way to hydrate the vocal cords instantly. Well, guess what? There is! It's called mist inhaling.

INHALING MIST

When I had strep throat, I decided to try using a popular sore throat spray. I was spraying my throat when I accidentally breathed in at the same time. Although I coughed, gagged, and wheezed, I finally experienced some relief from my pain. By breathing in while spraying, I inhaled the mist down my trachea, which coated and numbed my vocal cords. Although I wouldn't recommend inhaling a throat spray, it did give me an idea.

When I recovered from strep throat, I decided to try this with plain water. I filled up a 1-ounce mist bottle and mist inhaled during practice. I felt like I could sing forever. Inhaling mist immediately lubricates the vocal cords by direct contact. I use this practice every time I sing. If you want to do the same, I suggest a bottle small enough to keep in your pocket.

When first learning to mist-inhale, I suggest that you breathe in lightly. If you don't inhale lightly at first, you might choke. Don't worry, you aren't going to drown, but you do need to get used to the feeling of having water applied to your vocal cords. After a few tries, you can breathe in deeper, to really moisten the cords. I usually mist inhale about three times in a row, in between songs. So as a general guide, you should drink water regularly throughout your performance, mist-inhale between songs, and if needed, take a little mist-inhale during the guitar solo.

GARGLING WATER

Another effective method for hydrating the vocal cords is gargling with water. Gargling vibrates and massages the throat muscles, much like relaxing in a whirlpool. Gargling allows a small amount of water to trickle down to the vocal cords, helping to moisten them. Gargling is such a relaxing exercise for the voice that I use it as an exercise during my warm-up and exercise routines and during singing. Only gargle with water at room temperature to avoid shocking the vocal cords.

Now do you understand why water is such an important part of every vocalist's life? Not only does water hydrate the voice, but it also keeps your body healthy. Always do everything possible to keep your voice healthy. Singing is demanding on the entire body. If a guitar player breaks a string, he can replace it. If you don't take care of your voice, you'll eventually blow it out, and you won't find any throats on sale at your local music store. So if you aren't very fond of water, you had better learn to love it. There is no exception to this rule.

Useful Tip: The Importance of Water-
*If you are interested in learning more about the importance that water plays in the functioning of the body, you should read "**Your Body's Many Cries For Water**" and "**You're Not Sick, You're Thirsty**" by **F. Batmanghelidj, M.D.***

RAISE YOUR VOICE

Useful Tip: Massaging the Voice via Sound & Water-

This is an effective method for "massaging" the vocal cords via sound that I learned from a throat specialist that can be accomplished with the assistance of water. Purchase a ¾-1-1/2 inch in diameter piece of flexible tubing, approximately 2-3 feet in length, from a local hardware store. This is like the tubing used for fish aquariums. Put one end of the tubing in your mouth and the other end into a bucket of water. Begin humming into the tube until the water bubbles from the sound. The tone will carry down the tubing and into the water. The sound waves will reverberate back up the tubing and down the trachea until the waves come, once again, in contact with their source of origin- the vocal cords. If you are experiencing a sore throat or the vocal cords are swollen from vocal abuse, this technique will lightly "massage" the vocal cords and help to relieve vocal stress.

Useful Tip: Diluting the Vocal Cords-

If your voice is dry and you've got to hit the stage soon, then it's time to dilute the vocal cords. Starting approximately an hour before performing, you must do the following-First, mix a cup of hot (not too hot) water with two tablespoons of honey. Try sipping your "honey tea" during the first 10 minutes. This will warm and relax the pharynx and allow quicker absorption of water into the throat lining. Next, you must drink AT LEAST 32 ounces of room temperature water over the next hour. Yes, I know, your gonna have to pee a lot. Oh well, that's the price you must pay. Run around on stage a lot and you'll sweat it out, so that you don't have to run back stage every five minutes to relieve yourself. Next, get a towel, and do a quick steam session over a water faucet. Breathe steam for at least 5-10 minutes-in through the nose and out through the mouth. You should be working on drinking your 32 ounces as well. When you have finished streaming, you should still have about 40 minutes left until performing. I'm assuming you are going to start warming up now. 40 minutes should be plenty of time for warming up, with a few minutes to spare. Start your mist inhaling regimen as soon as you start warming up- mist inhale in between your exercises and every 5 minutes. Don't forget to take drinking water with you on stage (as well as your misting bottle). Now you're ready for an awesome show!

7 The Importance Of Pitch

One of the key elements to becoming a great singer is *intonation*. Intonation is the ability to hear and sing in tune. If a singer cannot sing in tune, your ears will suffer. Many singers are out of tune without realizing it. For some reason, singing off-key is a problem that many singers overlook. Poor intonation could stem from not paying attention. If you don't support the tone, your pitch will go flat. If you incorrectly push too hard with your stomach muscles, forcing the air pressure, the tone will sound forced, you'll strain, and the pitch will go sharp. This can be taxing on the vocal cords. But more importantly, poor intonation could stem from poor listening habits, or an untrained ear.

The best way to learn to sing in tune is by *pitch matching*. Pitch matching is vocally matching notes to a fixed note instrument. It is probably best to use an electronic keyboard. This is a far better choice than a guitar or an actual piano. Guitar strings have a tendency to go flat, and the piano might not be properly tuned. A keyboard will stay true to pitch.

When you start this exercise, hit any note on the keyboard that is comfortable for your vocal range, and then vocally try to sustain the same note. Repeat the process several times for different pitches in your range. In order to follow the notes you are sustaining, you should learn the names of the notes of the keyboard.

If you are not sure that you are correctly matching the note, an *electronic tuner* might be of some benefit. An electronic tuner is simply a small hand-held device that reads a pitch and tells whether the pitch is sharp or flat. You can purchase one from your local music store ($20-$100).

Play a note on the keyboard, let's say a middle C, and turn on the tuner to check and see that the keyboard is tuned. Next, play a note on the keyboard and vocally match the same pitch with the tuner on. The tuner will show you how close you are to the correct pitch. You'll either need to pull back on breath support if the note is sharp, or, if the note is flat, add a little more support to match the note and make the tuner read in tune.

Matching pitch is also an internally mental vocal cord adjustment. In time, with practice, it will become second nature to you.

Next, hit any note on the keyboard, visualize the note, and then vocally match it. Check the tuner to see how close you were. If you weren't perfectly in tune, do not release the note. Adjust the pitch accordingly. Once you've matched the pitch, notice how it feels to sustain that perfectly tuned note. It should feel natural and effortless.

THE PITCH WHEEL

Another tool for pitch perfection is the *pitch wheel*. A pitch wheel is a small round hand-held instrument, much like a harmonica, which covers one chromatic octave. Pitch wheels come in several different keys. If you plan to purchase one, I suggest a pitch wheel in the key of C for males and a pitch wheel in the key of F for females. The pitch wheel in the key of C covers an octave starting at middle C, or C4 up to Tenor high C, or C5. The pitch wheel in the key of F covers an octave starting on F4 above middle C, up to F5, in the Alto range. A pitch wheel is much cheaper than a keyboard or tuner ($10-$20). It fits easily into your pocket and doesn't need batteries. It is the perfect instrument for your vocal workout. I use a pitch wheel for my exercise program, so I'd suggest purchasing one soon.

TUNING YOUR INSTRUMENT

Yes, singers everywhere, you do have an instrument…your voice! You can tune this instrument, just like any other. Recently, a student of mine pointed out an interesting concept. You can improve your intonation by humming into the pitch wheel. (Thanks, Mark.) Blowing into a hole on the pitch wheel causes a small copper reed to vibrate to the pitch that is stamped above that hole. If you hum into the hole, instead of blowing, the reed will vibrate just the same. The reed will always vibrate to the true pitch. If you aren't humming in tune with the same pitch, the combination of pitches will sound sour. As you adjust the pitch of your voice, the sound will eventually become sweet and resonant. When the two pitches are out of tune you will hear a series of vibrating sound waves. As you approach perfect pitch, the waves will smooth out. When you have matched the pitch of the reed, you have tuned your instrument to the correct pitch. Be for- warned, your cords are more like guitar strings than a pitch wheel, so you could still go sharp or flat. **Pitch Wheel Demonstration**

Singing in tune harmonizes with your own natural frequencies, which creates more resonant sensations within your voice and body. Every living thing vibrates, and is tuned to a particular frequency. In fact, your body is a finely tuned instrument in its own right. Your body knows when you are singing in tune. True pitch comes easier when you are relaxed, and will have a deeper sounding resonation within your body.

As you learn to sing and sustain notes in tune, you'll discover that each individual note will have a slightly different feeling than any other note. Your body will set these physical feelings to memory, and you will be able to use these feelings guide to help keep you in tune. Another way to stay in tune is described in the next chapter.

Useful Tip: Time to Listen to Yourself-

Try recording yourself singing along with one of your favorite songs. As you listen back, pay close attention to your pitch as opposed to the actual singer. How does it sound? If it sounds sour and doesn't mix well with the original artist, keep practicing matching pitches. You goal is to make it to sound like a mini-choir or a perfectly tuned duet.

RAISE YOUR VOICE

8 Listening On The Inside (The Inner Voice)

It can be a real battle to hear yourself while you are singing. If you have to compete with a band, or members of a chorus, this could prove to be difficult. If you are struggling to hear yourself, you might be singing louder than you should. Singing too loudly (for the sake of being heard) by forcing the sound is damaging to your voice. It is difficult enough for a singer to distinguish how he or she truly sounds, without the added noise. Just try recording yourself sometime, if you haven't already. I bet that you'll be surprised to find out that you sound quite a bit different than you actually thought you did.

As you sing, the sound is carried outward, away from your body. Your ears cannot pick up on the true quality of your own voice. One way to hear your true sound is to cup your ear and pull it down towards your mouth. Just wrap your fingers around the back of the ear, and slightly pull your ear forward, toward your mouth. This is a trick I picked up on my own a few years ago when I was competing with a rock band to hear myself. They had a loud P.A. system, but poor monitors.

Depending upon the loudness of your voice and your hand positioning, the volume might be too loud for your ears. Play around with your hand positioning until the sound is comfortable. The closer you pull your ear towards your mouth, the greater amplified the sound. This little trick allows your ears to pick up on the vibrations as they come out of you.

Cupping your ears can benefit you in several ways:

- This can help to correct your pitch.
- It is a lot easier to sing in tune when you can hear yourself.
- When you hear mistakes, you can correct them.
- This will show you how truly powerful your voice can be.
- This will let you know when to back off your volume.
- This will help you to avoid straining.

• It's useful when playing live and you are having trouble hearing yourself.

• You can cup one ear with one hand while holding your microphone in your other hand.

• Nobody will notice what you are doing.

As I said before, in time you'll learn to distinguish the true sound of your voice. Not only will you be able to physically feel and hear the tone, but mentally able to hear and feel the tone as well. Cupping your ears can be your best friend and teacher, as well as your worst critic. You'll discover all of the beautiful qualities of your voice, as well as all of your flaws, but this will only help you to correct them. Master this invaluable little trick and make it a permanent part of your singing career.

Useful Tip: In-ear Monitors-

Tony Harnell *offers another solution: "I recommend that all professional singers try using in-ear monitors. They are hard to get used to, but if you take the time to work with the engineer, and get a good mix of the band, it will be well worth it. When you go from gig to gig, the monitors change all the time and the rooms are always different. By using in-ears, you'll get the same sound, no matter what. In hard rock, it can be very loud on stage. Most guitarists won't turn down, so you need to have control over your own volume."*

9 Developing Style

The best way to develop style is by singing along with other singers. You'll benefit by listening to vocalists that sing the songs you love. Choose the singers that inspire you. Buy their CD's and learn to sing every song. Analyze your favorite singer's voice. Work on perfecting the part of their technique that you admire, whether it is their vibrato, lyrical phrasing, or emotions they evoke through the sound of their voice.

However, **do not ever try to completely copy a singer**. A singer's distinct sound quality is due to the physical makeup of that individual's voice. Trying to mimic your favorite singer is virtually impossible, and possibly harmful. **Forcing your voice to sound a certain way can cause you to strain**. You want to emulate a singer's taste, not his or her exact sound. Learn from your favorite singers then build on your own true style. Have confidence in your own voice, and your own style.

I once knew a guy who tried so hard to perfectly emulate the sound of **Sebastian Bach**, (original singer of **Skid Row**), that he would constantly lose his voice. **Sebastian** is an amazing vocalist. So, not only was my friend trying to emulate an amazing voice, he was dealing with a singer who also possessed great technique. His vocal makeup wasn't even close to **Sebastian's** voice. His outlook was, "If he can sound that way, so can I." The last I had heard, he wasn't singing anymore, due to vocal problems.

The only exceptions to this rule are singers in *tribute bands*. Tribute bands are cover bands that emulate a specific band. They try to copy the band as much as possible, from the clothes they wear, to the instruments they play, to perfecting the band's sound. In this case you are intentionally trying to sound like that singer. Trying to sound like a particular singer isn't always a good idea.

As I said, this can be harmful to your voice. Lead singers of tribute bands usually already have a physical vocal makeup very similar to the singers they are emulating. If you naturally sound a lot like a particular singer, this might be a job opportunity for you. In fact, there are several professional bands that have continued on with new lead singers that sound very similar to the original singer. **Journey** is a band that has successfully continued on with a new singer that fit the bill.

Useful Tip: Finding Your Niche-

*I use to love to sing songs by 80's rock group **Journey**, but hard as I tried, I couldn't sound anything like **Steve Perry**. I wanted to sound like **Perry** more than anything, but it just wasn't going to happen. I finally found my niche' the first time I sang **Immigrant Song** by **Led Zeppelin**. Finally, everything seemed to fit and vocally flow. For me, stylistically, that's who I am. I'm not saying that I sound like **Robert Plant**, because I don't. But, that was the first rock song that gave me freedom and allowed my voice to open up. I could sing **Immigrant Song** much easier than I could ever sing **Separate Ways**, although **Immigrant Song** was higher pitched. It wasn't about the pitch-it was about the tonality. The way in which **Plant** tonally and stylistically sang that song, is the tonality and style that fits me as a vocalist. You'll know when you find a song that fits you, because it will physically and mentally feel right. Keep singing and you'll eventually find your niche'.*

Every famous singer has copied another singer in one way or another. How did they learn to sing? They learned by singing along with other people's songs. Instead of parroting their idols, they took bits and pieces of their favorite vocalist's vocal tricks and put them into their own little bag of vocal tricks. Then they applied what they'd learned to their own style. If you ever get a chance to meet one of your favorite singers, ask them who influenced them vocally. Then see if you can hear any similarities in their voices.

My favorite singers are too numerous to mention. If I were to write all of their names down, it would fill this entire chapter. (**Jim Gillette, Tony Harnell, Miljenko Matijevic, Terry Ilous, Sahaj Ticotin, Rob Thomas, Ray West, Prince, Mark Slaughter, Sting, Marq Torien, Seal, Joe Elliot, Ray Gillen, Ian Thornley, Chris Cornell, Jeff Buckley, Erik Rogers, Josey Scott, David Draiman, Geoff Tate, Simon Lebon, Tyler Connely, Steve Augeri, Rob Halford, Michael Bolton, Myles Kennedy, Alanis Morissette, Amy Lee, Robert Plant, Melvin Riley, Brian Johnson, Lajon Witherspoon, Chester Bennington, John Secada, Steven Tyler, Brent Smith, Phil Tayler, Shaun Morgan, Peter Cetera, James Labrie, Lenny Wolf** and **Steve Perry** to name a few.)

I have been influenced in some way by just about everybody I've ever heard, whether it was a certain tone in a singer's voice that moved me or something in a singer's voice that I didn't particularly like. In that case I would make sure to try not to repeat the same mistakes in my own singing. I have tried to learn from every singer I have ever heard. In some way or another, I combine a little bit of each of my favorite singer's style with my own style. So don't be afraid to sing along with your favorite singers. It will help you to create your own identity.

Useful Tip: Open Your Mind To Other Singers and Styles-

*While working on developing your own style, don't limit yourself to just singing songs by your favorite artists only. Try broadening your horizons by listening to other artists and styles. I recently bought CD's by **Edguy, Primal Fear, Seal** and **Clay Aiken**. Although, bands like **Edguy** and **Primal Fear** are styles that I am very familiar with, it was new material for me to sing. Listening to **Seal** helped me to focus on a smoky, calm and controlled type tone, while listening to **Clay Aiken** enabled me to work on a pure open mid-range, mixed voice tone. You can apply qualities from other styles to ANY STYLE you wish to sing! Open your mind!*

Useful Tip: Don't Forget the Low Notes!

*If your goal is to sing songs above your range, don't forget the low notes! You've got to work out your ENTIRE range. So, if you are a rock singer and you've only been singing along with bands like **Shinedown, RA** or **Alter Bridge,** for the last three months, try adding songs from bands with lower range singers, like **Three Doors Down, Tool,** or **No Address**. Try to find a low range singer that is just as challenging for you as the high-end singers. Look for notes BELOW your range. Your goal should be to extend your range in both directions!*

Useful Tip: What Would My Favorite Singer Do?

*I want you to imagine that one of you favorite singers has magically switched places with you, and is now trapped inside of your body, like in the movie **Freaky Friday**. If your favorite singer is **Amy Lee** from **Evanescence**, or **Shaun Morgan** from **Seether**, I want you to ask yourself this question- " how would **Amy** or **Shaun** suddenly approach singing with your body and vocal cords (without forcing himself to sound like he did in his own body)?" Now, try singing a few of that artist's songs. You see, singing isn't just about what **GOD** has given you-it's about your perception of voice. I'm sure that many of the professional singers that you love, would still have done well with a different set of vocal cords, because they would have used their perception of voice to mold the voice they wanted.*

Part Two Vocal Health

Keeping the voice in perfect health is an all-day, everyday job. Daily exercise, proper breath technique, and drinking plenty of water are all important parts of vocal health, but there are many other aspects involved as well. You need to live your life as a singer. No matter your profession, you are a singer above all else. Keep this in mind the next time you decide to shout at a ball game, smoke, constantly clear your throat, or any other voice-hampering compromise.

We live in a society of excess. Whatever you excessively put into your body affects your voice. Maintaining a healthy voice comes with compromise. Alcohol, tobacco, and junk food negatively affect your voice, while fresh fruits and vegetables, vitamins and minerals, and water help to create a healthy environment within the body.

The following sections delve into different aspects of vocal health. **Chapter 10, The SPEAKING VOICE**, approaches the misuse of everyday speaking and how this can affect the singing voice. **Chapter 11, MENTAL INHIBITION** deals with the mental side of singing and how to overcome a negative attitude. **Chapter 12, AILMENTS OF THE VOICE** deals with the physical ailments of the body and how to deal with them. **Chapter 13, ENEMIES OF THE VOICE** discusses substances that have been proven harmful to the voice. **Chapter 14, THE SINGER'S MEDICINE CHEST**, presents a list of vitamins, minerals, and herbs that help to promote a strong and healthy vocal mechanism. **Chapter 15, THE SINGER'S DAILY REGIMEN**, presents a list of nutrients that, if taken daily, are beneficial to maintaining a singer's health.

> *DISCLAIMER: The following sections are not intended to prescribe, treat, prevent or diagnose any illness. Consult your physician before taking any of the following vitamins, minerals, or herbs.*

RAISE YOUR VOICE

10 The Speaking Voice

Do you wish to have a long successful vocal career? Then correct your speaking voice by eliminating poor vocal habits. If you wish to incorporate any of the following vocal habits into your singing, do so with care. You know your voice and know what you are capable of doing. Continual use of any of these vocal habits could produce *vocal nodules*. Vocal nodules are calluses on the vocal cords due to abuse of the voice. Although there is a chance that a node can be reversed and disappear with vocal rehabilitation, usually they can only be removed by surgery.

The speaking and singing voice are one and the same. The way you speak affects the way you sing. Many singers don't take the time to protect and care for their instrument. You must treat your voice with respect. If a guitarist had to carry their instrument around with them all day, they would be very cautious. They would keep their instrument in a case to ensure that it is kept out of harm's way. The difference between a guitarist and a singer is; guitarists view themselves as musicians and treat their instrument with respect, whereas most singers don't respect the fact that their voice is their instrument. Few singers give their voice the care and respect that it deserves. Since you can't stick your voice in a case, you need to find other means of protecting it.

First, you must start viewing yourself as a singer, and finally realize that **your voice is your instrument**! You must learn how to protect and care for your voice. One way to protect your singing voice is to evaluate your speaking voice. It is possible that you are abusing your speaking voice during everyday conversation. The problem with poor speaking habits is that the strain of everyday speaking affects your singing voice. To evaluate your own voice, you must familiarize yourself with several different types speaking habits. The following is a list of abusive vocal patterns that should be corrected and avoided.

VOICE TYPES

People drop the tone of their voice a few notes lower than is necessary, producing *too low a pitch for their voice.* The tone sounds big and has a forced feeling. I know many male singers who feel that this big masculine tone is what makes you a man. Guys, please, learn to speak with your real voice, even if it is lighter and higher. I promise that it doesn't make you any less of a man. If you adopt this vocal pattern, you will only limit the range of your voice.

Some people raise their pitch higher than necessary producing *too high a pitch for their voice*. This is usually an attempt to sound more delicate and feminine. This only thins out the quality of the speaking voice. I've heard both male and female singers speak like this and it reminds me of a child's voice. I'm no psychiatrist, but I feel that the individual is hanging on to childhood for some reason, whether for attention or the fear of growing up. If you feel that this pertains to you, then figure out and face the problems that are keeping you locked inside of a child's voice.

I've also noticed that some people tend to speak with a *breathy voice,* or, as I've heard it called, the *sexy voice*. Typically, a breathy sound is associated with a sexy tone; the breathy voice presents a certain aura of sexuality. Think of **Marilyn Monroe**. The sexy voice can also be accompanied with a vocal fry type sound. This is the sound your voice makes when you first wake up in the morning and it sounds throaty or groggy. Adding breath or vocal fry to your speaking voice will dry out and irritate the vocal cords. Just the opposite of a breathy tone is a *tone with little breath support*. This occurs when you hold your breath. The tone can sound pinched, almost grunt-like, and can be as irritating on the vocal cords as using too much breath. Without enough breath for speech, the vocal cords will have to try to compensate for insufficient breath and may become swollen from the irritation.

Useful Tip: Don't Hold Your Breath!

Start paying attention to your breathing habits during speech. Are you holding your breath? Don't lock your stomach when you breathe. Are you breathing with your stomach? Don't hold the stomach in, out of fear that someone will see your stomach sticking out. Don't raise your shoulders or breathe with your upper chest when you speak. Are you using too much air? You must focus on moderation and breath consistency. Breath release should be very natural. Take a sufficient breath and say what you have to say. You don't have to have a full breath to say three words, and you don't have to try to fit thirty words into one breath. Become a moderate paced speaker; approximate each breath for each sentence.

A *monotone voice* is one that retains the same pitch, whether low or high, while speaking. Constantly speaking on the same pitch is unhealthy and straining on the vocal cords. Monotone speaking weakens the elasticity of the cords. You are inhibiting your vocal cords from properly stretching and zipping. To understand what this sounds like, repeat the previous three sentences while maintaining the same pitch. A monotone voice is so dull and unpleasant. This always reminded me of one of my math teachers in middle school. No wonder I kept falling asleep in class. Ha-ha.

RAISE YOUR VOICE

The sound of a *raspy* or *husky voice* resembles a grunting sound with a lot of air behind it. This is harsh on the vocal cords because, by tightening the cords to produce this tone, you are using too much air, which has a drying effect on your voice and could result in vocal cord swelling. As you lightly grunt, repeat the last few sentences. The sound is breathy, tight, and pinched in the throat. **Rod Stewart** has a naturally husky voice and it is apparent when he speaks and sings.

Personally, when people tell me that they are naturally husky, I don't buy it. I don't believe that anyone is naturally raspy or husky. Unless there is a vocal deformation or problem, it's probably just the result of poor speaking habits.

A more intense throaty version of this vocal type produces a *gravelly voice*. The sound produced by this vocal type is similar to a growl or a low- pitched version of screaming, which has been made popular by new-metal bands like **Lamb of God** and **Shadows Fall**. It sounds throaty and can be damaging to your vocal cords, forcing excessive air pressure past the vocal cords. However, as far as singing this way, there is an art to this type of singing and it can be done successfully through proper voice placement and correct tightening of the stomach.

Screaming incorporates the previous vocal types to the extreme. Many heavy metal singers incorporate screaming into their style of singing. Screaming is an art form and can be done correctly. Some veteran heavy metal singers are still performing; some had short-lived careers due to the pressures of singing. One exception that comes to mind is **Brian Johnson**, lead singer of **AC/DC**. His singing style incorporates the three previous vocal types, and when he speaks, his voice is raspy. The reason his voice is raspy, is because he is speaking from his lower throat-he is allowing the sound to drop down into the throat which causes the cords to rub together like a vocal fry. Speaking from the lower throat is vocal suicide, but, by some miracle, he has been able to continue this vocal approach for years, and is still going strong. **David Draiman** of **Disturbed** has an incredible voice. He can growl, scream, and is still able to sing as smooth as silk. He continues to tour and sing in this manner with no trouble at all. But, when he talks his voice is very clean.

If you want to sing this way you must make absolutely sure that you don't tighten your throat. If you do, you'll only harm your voice. The only way to scream or sing throaty is to sing with a very open throat. You've got to keep the throaty sound off of the vocal cords and up towards the soft palate. If you have to tighten your throat, like grunting, then you are doing it wrong. You've got to keep the back of the throat open wide, like yawning. There is definitely a technique to screaming, or how else could **Chester Bennington** of **Linkin Park** play 320+ shows in one year.

A *nasal voice* is produced when you project too much of the sound up into your nose instead of out through your mouth. Pinch your nose shut and repeat the last sentence. Notice how the sound becomes nasal, with very little resonance. **Fran Drescher** from the sitcom, **The Nanny**, speaks very nasal, but it has become her trademark sound. **Mark Slaughter** has an incredible voice and sings very nasal, but the nasality works very well in his style of singing. There is nothing wrong with a slight nasality when you speak, but too much is ear pollution. A *whiney voice* incorporates nasality with higher, thinner pitches (child like voice). As you speak with a whine you will have a tendency to change and raise the pitch of your voice on individual words. This results in a lack of clarity and focus.

DYNAMICS

Dynamics affect your voice as well. Dynamics, as previously explained, refers to how soft or loud the volume of your voice. Speaking *too loudly* will strain your vocal cords. If you are speaking too loudly, you are most likely incorrectly tightening the stomach muscles, thus applying too much air pressure against the vocal cords. Screaming is produced in the same manner. Abusing your voice in this manner could result in a sore throat, or vocal nodules. You might speak this way in a crowd to be heard. To increase volume, you should rely more on resonance expansion as opposed to tightening the stomach for volume. **The sole purpose of the stomach muscles as applied to singing, is breath support, not volume support.**

Useful Tip: Take It Outside-
*Now that I've said my peace, if you do need to tighten the stomach, remember, the only correct way to tighten the stomach is to use the **Power Push**, which will be explained at the end of the book. If you are in a crowd and need to talk, and if the conversation is that important, go somewhere quiet or take it outside, where you can easily be heard.*

On the other hand you may be *speaking too softly*. People will have trouble understanding or hearing you. The softer you speak, the closer you are to approaching a *whisper*. A whisper is the quietest, breathiest sound you can produce. Whispering is fine in moderation, but the continual allowance of extra breath flow past the vocal cords only dries out the throat. In this situation, you must focus on breath support as well as resonance expansion for a fuller sound.

I recently had a young girl come to me because she was in charge of a marching band and needed more volume. The band complained because they couldn't hear her. She was speaking so softly that I had to have her speak into my ear at the beginning of her vocal training. She wasn't supporting her voice correctly and was using too much breath, like whispering. With an hour of training, I was able to bring her out of her shell.

ENUNCIATION

Proper enunciation is very important in everyday conversation. Mumbling or slurring your words creates problems in communication. (Many songs are inaudible because of slurring: **Jimi Hendrix'** *Purple Haze*, **Dobey Grey's** *Give Me the Beat*, and *Louis, Louis,* by the **Kingsman**. It's irritating not to be able to understand the lyrics of a song. E-NUN-CI-A-TION is the key people. I have several students who tend to mumble their words when they sing, so, I'll make them open and close their mouth as wide as possible, as they sing each vowel and consonant. After a few songs of over-enunciation, the problem is usually overcome.

Stuttering affects many people. There are books on proper enunciation that might help, or you may wish to contact a speech therapist. You might decide to contact a voice specialist for any of the above vocal habits.

TO SHOUT OR WHISPER?

Shouting adds an undue amount of breath pressure on the vocal cords. Massive bursts of air are as bad as coughing. Shouting for an extended period of time will result in the loss of your voice. It could take several days before your voice returns to normal. **Shouting is vocal suicide for a singer!**

On the opposite end of the scale is whispering. Most people think that whispering is a way to give your voice a break. This is wrong! If you have a sore throat, the best way to rest your voice is not to speak. Whispering can be just as damaging as if you were shouting. **A whisper is a quiet shout.** Whispering irritates the cords and it will take longer for the cords to heal.

USE YOUR TRUE VOICE!

The best speaking voice to use is your own natural voice. Aim for a clear resonant voice, focused in the mask. What is the mask? The mask is a term used hundreds of years ago, when actors would wear masks during a performance. In order to be heard and for the sound to carry, the singer would have to focus the sound forward, toward the nose and cheeks. If you keep a buzzing sensation in the teeth, and place the sound of your voice up into the sinuses and cheeks, you'll produce a clear, full, ringing tone. **Sahaj Ticotin** of **RA** has a clear, resonant voice when he sings. He speaks very clearly as well, so I'm sure he'll have a long vocal career. Considering that your singing and speaking voice are the same, you should also apply the vocal techniques from this book to your speaking voice as well. The **core of resonance** and **resonance expansion** visualizations should always be applied. You want to feel and hear the affects of resonance in your voice and body.

Useful Tip: Taste The Sound-
Think about what it tastes like to have a mouth full of cotton candy. When you sing, you want the color of your voice to fill your mouth with resonance, just like a mouth full of cotton candy. Filling the mouth with resonance and tasting the sound is one of the keys to effortless singing!

I know that it's difficult to continue visualizations throughout the day, but you should maintain an awareness of what is physically going on with your voice. When you perform, you wouldn't sing the entire song monotone. So why would you speak this way? My friends call me the walking vocal exercise, because when I talk, I vary the pitch of my voice from low to high.

Varying the pitch of your voice throughout the day continually stretches and zips the vocal cords to different positions. This strengthens the voice and works your vocal range, which keeps the voice healthy by increasing lubrication to the vocal cords. If you constantly speak at the same pitch, you tire and strain the vocal cords. If the pitch is varied, a signal is sent to the brain, sending notification that the cords are stretching to different positions and require more lubrication. As you perform, you may add any of these voice types for the purpose of variance in your singing style. However, you would not continue to sing the entire song with any one of these vocal inflections. You should aim for a resonant, clean tone when you sing. You want to aim for the same clean, vibrant tone when you speak as well.

Useful Tip: The Laughing Voice-

How do I know if I'm using the correct tone? I think about my laughing voice. When you laugh, your voice floats forward towards the front of your face in little resonant bursts, (unless of course, you have some weird laugh like a horse, hyena, or, or pig. Ha-ha.) You should feel the sound in the area known as the mask; feel the teeth, cheeks, and nose buzz, and taste the sound as well. My wife says that I laugh like a penguin, but the sound is very forward and resonant. When I feel my voice slipping into my throat, I focus on applying my "laughing voice." NO BREATHINESS PLEASE!

To discover your true speaking voice, record yourself as you read out loud. As you listen back to the recording, check your vocal habits. Is the pitch too low, too high, or monotone? Is the sound of your voice whiney or nasal? Is it throaty, or breathy? Does it sound forward, or sound like it is stuck in the back of the throat? When you realize and understand your own speaking patterns, you can correct your voice by eliminating poor speaking habits. It could take several weeks before your voice will adjust to these newly adopted vocal patterns. After you feel you have adjusted your speaking voice, repeat the recording process. As you record yourself, it is best not to think about vocal correction. Just read aloud and let your voice guide itself. By doing this, you will know what vocal habits have been eliminated, and which problems still need worked on. If you are going to be a great singer, then you must take care of your speaking voice. This is the only physical instrument that you'll ever possess. Taking care of your speaking voice can add years to your singing career!

Useful Tip: The Authority on the Speaking Voice!

*Do you want to learn more about how to correctly use and find your true speaking voice? World Renowned voice pathologist, **Dr. Morton Cooper**, is the leading expert on the subject. He is the ONLY doctor ever proven to naturally cure Spasmodic Dysphonia (strangled voice), and has helped singers and speakers to reverse vocal nodules WITHOUT surgery! He is the author of "**Change Your Voice, Change Your Life**", "**Winning With Your Voice**", and "**Stop Committing Vocal Suicide.**" Developing your correct speaking voice should be the #1 priority for any serious vocalist. **Dr. Morton Cooper** is the right choice!*

Useful Tip: Other Speaking Resources-

*Here are a few other resources for exercising the speaking voice-**Thomas Appell's, "The Secrets To Successful Speaking**, is a free bonus CD that is included with his book, "**Can You Sing A High C Without Straining.**" This CD presents exercises and tips for developing your speaking voice. **Roger Love's, "Vocal Power"**, is a 6 CD set that presents the listener with explanations and corrections for poor speaking habits. **Roger** has also included a bonus DVD with the "**Vocal Power**" set.*

RAISE YOUR VOICE

11 Mental Inhibition

What you can imagine you can accomplish. Singing is both a physical and mental process. Visualization can help the voice to flow freely, but can work both positively and negatively. If you think negative thoughts about yourself and your singing, it will show in your voice. Developing negative thought patterns will inhibit your progression as a singer. Never finish a negative thought or sentence about yourself or your singing. Turn the thought or phrase into a positive visual or statement. If you think, "I will never be able to sing three notes higher," then I can almost guarantee that you will never increase your range by three notes. Change the sentence into something positive, such as, "With time and practice my range will increase." Repeat the phrase throughout the day to affirm your goal and diminish the negative thought. Always turn a negative statement around to create a positive phrase.

I didn't break a glass by voice alone for the 1ˢᵗ 6 weeks of trying, but I kept affirming that I could until I did!

Repetitive positive statements are referred to as *affirmations*. The more you repeat an affirmation the deeper it is imprinted upon your subconscious. Your mind eventually accepts the statement as true and works toward manifesting the affirmation as reality. This is the reason that negative statements are dangerous to your progress. The subconscious is just like a very young child; it doesn't differentiate between positive and negative, it only follows orders. So, be careful what you think.

If you want to help your vocal progress, you might want to create a few affirmations to add to your daily regimen. Before your vocal workout, you could try these affirmations: "The more I sing, the more my voice flows with beauty, freedom, strength, and grace," or, " My voice is a fluid, flawless instrument." Before a performance you could repeat the following: "The longer I sing, the stronger my voice becomes," and, "My performance is perfect." These affirmations help to assure that your voice doesn't tire as easily, because you will be focused on a positive outcome, which will prevent your nerves from taking over. I am always monitoring my body to make sure that I am singing correctly to prevent vocal stress and exhaustion. Affirmations work toward the same goal on a subconscious level. If I miss something, my subconscious is working to help correct my mistakes.

Be creative when writing your own personal affirmations. Your subconscious isn't stupid; so don't create unattainable affirmations. If you create an affirmation like, " I am the most incredible singer in the world," your mind will consider the affirmation a joke and you won't progress at all. Use common sense.

Another mental inhibition is *stage fright*. Stage fright is the fear of performing before an audience. Feeling nervous before a performance is not uncommon. Many well known singers have commented on stage fright in interviews. They have found ways to deal with their fears and so can you.

If you are developing fear or nervousness before performing, follow these three simple rules: **Breathe**, **Vocalize**, **Visualize:**

First re-establish your **breathing**. When the nerves kick in, your breathing speeds up. Deep breathing calms the nerves and relaxes the body. Try slowly inhaling through the nose and exhaling out through the mouth. Repeat the process 10 times. Next, **vocalize** by performing the exercises from the **Vocal Stress Release** program, which is explained in **Part Three** of this book. Nervousness tends to produce a shaky tone in your voice. By reconnecting to your voice, you help to eliminate the waiver. Finally, **visualize** a perfect performance and repeat some positive affirmations. Above all, believe in yourself.

This is the process I used when I was asked to appear on Good Morning America to see if I could shatter a glass with my voice… Did I shatter the glass with my voice? YES I DID!!!

Useful Tip: Mastering the Butterflies-

Learn to use stage fright to your advantage. Butterflies in the stomach can be a good-thing. It can bring forth the "Fight or Flight Response", which is a sudden rush of adrenaline in the body that occurs when you become extremely afraid or mad. Learn to use the butterflies in a positive way, like pumping yourself up for an awesome performance, instead of upsetting your stomach to the point of throwing up and mentally talking yourself out of singing. The choice is yours; you can either give the performance of a lifetime or clam up. The adrenaline rush is under your control; it will work either way you tell it to. So make it a positive. It's all in the way you perceive the situation.

Useful Tip: Learning To Focus-

Do you want to know the "secret" to successful visualization? All you need to do is close your eyes and focus ONLY on your desired result for four minutes! When I say focus, I mean hear it, think it, and see it in your mind…for four minutes!!! That's it! Sounds easy, doesn't it? Well, four minutes is tougher than it seems. If you can actually focus on your goal for four minutes without letting your mind drift to another subject and avoid the senseless thoughts that WILL drift into your mind, than you will accomplish your goal. When thoughts drift into your mind, let them float right out. I guarantee that you'll start thinking about things like, "I wonder what time it is", or, "what should I eat for dinner." So, set a timer, focus on your goal, and let the unimportant thoughts float right by!

Useful Tip: Step Inside Someone Else's Voice-

*This is a trick for stage fright that I used to help one of my students, **Josh Morrison**, open up and release the beautiful sound within him. **Josh** likes to sing songs by **John Mayer**. So, I told **Josh** to shut his eyes and pretend that **John Mayer** had a concert to perform but was too sick to sing. **John** then gave **Josh** his vocal cords and told him that he'd have to perform that night for him. So, **Josh** now had **John Mayer's** vocal cords and HAD to sing "**Mothers**" in front of thousands of people. What happened? How did he do? **Josh** gave me goose bumps when he sang that song. He finally made me believe him. He let go of himself and sang from the pure emotional part of the mind. Strange as it sounds, it works! Try it sometimes. (Sort of like "what would your favorite singer do?")*

Useful Tip: Know Who You Are!

*Fear and anxiety can affect you mentally and physically. The week before I flew to San Francisco to film the **MythBusters** episode, I became ill. I had been taking my usual supplements for vocal health, but, nonetheless, still developed a terrible cold. I couldn't even talk two days before my flight, and even considered canceling at the last minute. I arrived in San Francisco on February 7th, 2005, and went directly to bed. The next morning, when I arrived at the theater for the shoot, I was still hoarse, and my sinuses were clogged. If you listen to the way I sound on the show, you can tell that I had a sinus infection. So how did I deal with the situation? I realized that I was picked because I was considered the expert at breaking glasses. By that time, I had already broken 15 glasses. I walked up on to the stage and looked around the hall at the hundreds of empty seats. I realized that these seats were going to filled by millions of viewers. Associate producer **Linda Wolkovitch** asked me if I was nervous. My reply? "Nervous? Not at all. I'm home!" I knew I was ready and wouldn't let ANYTHING prevent me from succeeding! Believe and you WILL achieve!!!*

12 Ailments Of The Voice

The quality of your voice is affected by the health of your body. At some point in your life, I'm sure you will have to deal with at least a few of the following conditions. Although they might be unavoidable, here are some suggestions to help you deal with each situation:

ACID REFLUX

Acid reflux, also known as heartburn, is a condition in which stomach acid is forced up the esophagus, irritating the lining of the throat. Heartburn can be the result of poor eating habits and/or poor posture. If you gorge yourself every time you eat, you expand your stomach past the comfort zone. When the stomach cannot hold any more food, the hydrochloric acid in your stomach is forced up your throat. If you eat too quickly, not giving yourself enough time to properly chew your food, you are not aiding the digestion process. Chewing helps break down food, making it easier for your stomach to do its' job. Carbonated drinks can also expand your stomach. The fizz bubbles expand in your stomach resulting in the same situation.

Gastro Esophageal Reflux Disease (GERD), or now more commonly known as **Acid Reflux Disease** occurs when the valve between the stomach and the esophagus doesn't work properly. If the valve doesn't stay closed, stomach acid will back up the esophagus and irritate the throat lining. This is most noticeable at night while lying down. If you frequently wake up in the morning with a sore throat, you could be experiencing symptoms of **GERD**. Try elevating your head at night to alleviate the problem. Any over-the-counter stomach acid reducer could help control the problem by preventing the over-production of stomach acid. Try to avoid alcohol and caffeine; both weaken the valve. Avoid citrus fruits, tomatoes, and peppers, as well. These foods aggravate the situation.

If you experience heartburn, you might want to evaluate yourself. Do you have poor posture? If you do, then refer to the section on correcting your posture. Besides correcting your posture, you can perform the **Diaphragm Tension Release** exercise from the **Vocal Stress Release** program in **Part Three** of this book. This exercise returns the diaphragm to its natural position. When the diaphragm isn't tense, you will have less of a chance of experiencing heartburn.

Do you stuff yourself every time you eat? This is unhealthy. You are forcing your stomach to digest more than it can comfortably handle. Do you chew your food well or do you just inhale it? If food isn't broken down properly it could turn into body fat rather than energy. Besides heartburn, you will gain weight. So **quit gorging yourself!** Do you ever feel like you have to belch after drinking a soda pop? Try cutting back on carbonated drinks to see if this alleviates the problem. Sodas are loaded with caffeine, which aggravates heartburn. Spicy foods also aggravate heartburn. Take note of your eating and drinking habits.

There are many products on the market for heartburn. Calcium/Magnesium supplements work well. The Calcium helps restore the pH balance and the Magnesium has a relaxing effect on the stomach. If you are having trouble digesting your food, try a digestive aid like papaya enzyme tablets. Papaya tablets help break down food, minimizing the chance of heartburn. Another effective method is to add one to two tablespoons of apple cider vinegar to one cup of water. Apple cider vinegar aids digestion, relieves heartburn, and like Calcium, restores the pH balance to the body. If this drink is too bitter for your taste, try adding some honey to sweeten the mixture. If you feel that none of these symptoms pertain to you and you are still experiencing heartburn, contact your physician.

*My allergist put me on **Protonix** for acid reflux, which definitely helped. But, once I started paying attention to my diet and cut back on eating spicy foods, I noticed the problem disappeared, so I quit using **Protonix**.*

THE COMMON COLD

Nothing is worse than having to deal with a cold. Many singers refrain from singing (and speaking in some cases) with a cold, due to the fear of damaging their voices. Singing with a cold is quite possible, although uncomfortable. If you use proper vocal technique, your voice will be fine. A cold is an infection in the sinuses, the throat, or the lungs, or it could be a combination of all three.

An infection of the upper throat is referred to as *pharyngitis*. Your throat will be sore but you will still be able to speak or sing. Pharyngitis may be very painful, but as long as there is no infection in the vocal cords, you'll still be able to make it through a performance, although it won't feel that fun. Keep the sound out of the throat and focused into the resonant cavities of the head.

RAISE YOUR VOICE

The only time you should avoid speaking or singing is if you have *laryngitis*, which is an infection of the vocal cords. Your throat will feel swollen and sore. It could be so painful that you might not be able to speak. Swallowing will be difficult. The vocal cords are swollen due to the infection and enlarged blood vessels. In this state, the cords will not vibrate correctly

Do not speak or sing with laryngitis. You could damage your vocal cords. This includes whispering and gargling. Whispering is a quiet shout and gargling forces air past the irritated cords. The best remedy for laryngitis is plenty of water and absolute silence. Try a warm mist humidifier at night to moisten the air. Give your voice time to heal. Visit your doctor to see if antibiotics could help.

If you are developing a cold, this is a signal that your body is full of toxins and needs to cleanse itself of toxin overload. Once you notice cold symptoms developing, there are several things you can do to help the cleansing process along and shorten the duration of the cold:

When you notice the first signs of a cold: sore throat, congestion, coughing, etc., you must take immediate action. If you are under physical or mental stress, your body's supply of vitamin C and Calcium are being depleted. Both are important nutrients in fighting infection. At first sign of a cold, immediately increase your vitamin C and Calcium/Magnesium intake. Both can be purchased at any drug store. Magnesium helps to increase the body's absorption of Calcium, so it is wiser to take a combination of the two. Take 500 milligrams of vitamin C and 999 milligrams of Calcium every two hours until the symptoms start to diminish.

Zinc lozenges are beneficial during a cold. Zinc is proven to fight infection and to relieve a sore throat. An herbal combination of Goldenseal and Echinacea is excellent for fighting infection in the body. A few drops of Colloidal Silver under the tongue will be absorbed into the blood stream. Colloidal Silver is like a natural antibiotic and fights all forms of infection.

Useful Tip: I Shouldn't Be Telling You This-
Although I don't want to be known for recommending this, aspirin is a quick fix if you are set to do a gig and your voice is sore or swollen. Aspirin relieves aches and pains by thinning out the blood, making it easier for the blood to travel through constricted veins. It will help you to sing because it thins out the blood and reduces the swelling. Be forewarned, you could over sing and damage your voice without knowing it, because aspirin is only masking the symptoms.

Using aspirin is slightly, and I mean SLIGHLTY, similar to singers using cortisone shots in order to regain their voices for a gig (just not as damaging). As long as you are singing correctly, you should be fine. Don't make aspirin a habit. Aspirin also irritates the stomach lining, so never take it on an empty stomach. A few crackers will help.

Pneumonia is an infection of the lungs. If you feel you might have pneumonia, see your doctor. To break up chest congestion, tap repeatedly on your chest to loosen phlegm in your lungs. This will enable you to cough up and expel the mucus. Cup your hands and tap on your chest as if it were a drum. If you have someone tap on your back, the results will be better. Breathing steam or using a vaporizer helps to keep your lungs hydrated and will also loosen mucus.

Useful Tip: The Cold-Water Compress-
*A **cold-water compress** will help to draw out mucus from the lungs. To perform a cold-water compress, submerge a towel into a bowl of ice water. Wring out the towel and apply it to the front of your chest, then cover with a shirt and/or heavy blanket. Leave the towel on for fifteen to twenty minutes. Repeat the process three times. Perform this process three times on your back as well. This takes some time, but is quite effective. This process has always worked for me.*

Choose wisely any over-the-counter drugs you might take to fight a cold. Many only mask the symptoms, slowing down the healing process. There are several herbs listed in the next chapter that relieve pain, loosen congestion, and aid the healing process. A throat gargle is beneficial for a sore throat. These methods are discussed in the next few chapters. Now you have the means to fight off a cold.

CORTISONE SHOTS

The quick fix for touring singers who have lost their voice and still have to perform is taking cortisone injections in the throat. Cortisone is a nasty substance that immediately reduces the swelling of the vocal cords, making it easy to sing. I know several singers who have used cortisone shots to help them sing an important gig, including **Josey Scott** of **Saliva** and **James Labrie** of **Dream Theater**. The scary thing that both of these vocalists personally told me about cortisone shots, is the fact that you can sing like a bird afterwards, but don't feel a thing-you feel like you can do ANYTHING with your voice. Cortisone only temporarily eliminates the problem, and you can STILL do severe damage to your voice, because, like I said, you cannot feel anything.

COUGHING

Coughing is very harsh on the vocal cords. To demonstrate how coughing affects the vocal cords, fold a belt in two. Holding on to both ends, pull the belt apart. Notice how the belt made a loud smacking noise. Every time you cough you are smacking your vocal cords together in the same manner. Coughing causes the vocal cords to swell. If you must cough, then cough as lightly as possible. Clear your throat at a low volume to minimize damage. If you are only coughing to clear your throat, try humming on a low pitch instead. The low vibration helps to loosen the phlegm from the cords. There are times when coughing cannot be prevented. Drink plenty of water, breathe steam, rest your voice and try the following tips:

Useful Tip: An Alternative To Coughing-
Here's an easy way to remove thick mucus buildup from the vocal cords. Close your mouth and hum on a low note. Humming on low notes allows the vocal cords to vibrate without the restriction of vocal cord tension. After humming for a few moments, (which loosens vocal cord phlegm), suck on the inside of your lower lip, like sucking on a piece of hard candy. This works the muscles surrounding the vocal cords, to help break loose the phlegm, which has been loosened from humming. Then, lightly cough to expel the mucus. This is a much wiser choice than harshly coughing.

Useful Tip: Herbal Cough Syrup-
Any combination of the following herbs can be used to make a natural cough syrup, either by boiling the herb or adding 20-30 drops of the liquid extract to a cup of water:
__Licorice__ is an expectorant and soothes mucous membranes. __Mullein__ expels mucus and eases pain. Both __Slippery Elm__ and __Marshmallow__ root soothe the mucous membranes. __English Plantain__ is a natural cough suppressant. __Garlic__ helps to expel mucus. __Thyme__ is an expectorant and good for bronchitis. __Horehound__ soothes sore throats and, along with __Hyssop__ and __Lobelia__, a natural expectorant. __Peppermint__, although a natural form of menthol, will open the airways without drying out your throat.

DEHYDRATION

The body becomes dehydrated daily. You must replenish your body's water reserve every day. Working outside, especially in hot weather, will cause you to perspire more. When you perspire, you lose Sodium and Potassium, among other vitamins and minerals. Without Sodium, your body cannot fully process water. Potassium loss affects the muscles of the body, resulting in muscle cramping. Sodium and Potassium work together to maintain the pH balance in the body.

There are many signs of a dehydrated voice; your throat will be dry and might even ache. Your throat will feel tired and sound scratchy when you speak or sing. If you sing with dry cords, your voice will sound brittle, husky, and dull. There will be little resonance in your voice. This is most noticeable in the upper range. If you are experiencing any of these symptoms, you can bet your cords are somewhat dehydrated. The best solution is to drink lots of water and mist-inhale frequently.

EXHAUSTION

Lack of sleep can be very detrimental to a singer's health. In order to perform to the best of your ability, it is imperative that you get at least 8-10 hours of sleep every night. Singing is very demanding on the body. Without proper rest, your voice will suffer. Exhaustion will affect the quality of your voice and your range will shrink. I have interviewed dozens of singers, and the two most important things that singers always tell me that they require for their voice is plenty of water and plenty of sleep. Make sure that you are well rested before a performance, even if this means taking a nap several hours before.

SINUS TROUBLE

Signs of sinus trouble, or sinusitis, include sneezing, stuffiness, and postnasal drip. If the symptoms leave within a few weeks, then your sinus troubles were most likely the sign of a cold. If the symptoms persist, this might be a sign of allergies. If you feel this is possible, you might wish to consult an allergist for testing.

Sneezing is caused by an irritation of the sinus membranes. Sneezing is an involuntary muscular act produced by the body to expel the unwanted particle from the sinuses. Any small airborne particle inhaled through the nose can cause sneezing. Excessive sneezing is as damaging as coughing, forcing blasts of air from the lungs and slapping the vocal cords together. If you must sneeze, try to sneeze as non-vocal as possible. If you minimize sound production, you'll minimize vocal cord abuse. A *sinus flush* will help to relieve sneezing. In order to perform a sinus flush you will need salt, water, and a small rubber ear syringe. Mix one cup of warm water with a teaspoon of salt. The solution should be slightly salty to taste- too much salt can burn your sinuses. Fill the syringe with the water solution. Tilt your head back, then fill one nostril with the solution until the water flows from the other nostril. Repeat this several times in each nostril until the sinuses are clear.

The sinus flush breaks up hard, infected mucus and flushed unwanted particles from the sinus cavities. So don't freak out by what comes running out of your nostrils. Removing mucus restores the natural flow of the *cilia*. Cilia are tiny hairs that line the sinuses and throat and prevent small foreign particles from entering the lungs. When the cilia flow freely, sinus drainage returns to normal.

Sinus congestion is caused by the over-production of mucus in the sinus passages. Mucus builds up and hardens in the sinus cavities. This may be due to allergies or an irritation of the sinuses. Blowing your nose helps to remove mucus buildup. A sinus flush is very beneficial. Another beneficial exercise is the *sinus tension release.*

To perform this exercise, place your thumb and forefinger of either hand on the sides of the bridge of the nose. Squeeze the bridge of the nose for one second, and then release the pressure for one second. Repeat this process ten to fifteen times. This will open the sinuses for proper drainage. Massaging above and below the eyes will break up congestion as well.

Excessive sinus drainage, or *postnasal drip*, is also the result of allergies and sinus irritation. There is an over-production of mucus that must drain. Blowing the nose prevents mucus buildup. A sinus flush will help return healthy functioning. If allergies persist, whether housed in the sinuses or throat, consult an ear, nose, and throat doctor or a qualified allergist.

Useful Tip: Hum Your Way To Clear Sinuses-
Another effective technique to open the sinus passages is to hum "nnnnn" and allow the resonant sound to vibrate through the sinus cavities. Slide through your range on "nnnnn" until you find the pitch that is your "sweet spot"-the one pitch that vibrates heaviest in your sinus passages. When you find this pitch, close off one nostril at a time, then sustain "nnnnn" for as long as possible. One nostril is usually more congested than the other, so each nostril must be isolated as you do this exercise. It may take several minutes before the sinuses begin to open, but I assure you, this technique works!

RAISE YOUR VOICE

13 Enemies Of The Voice

ALCOHOL

Alcohol is a rapid dehydrator. To observe this, rub a little rubbing alcohol on your skin. It will evaporate quickly. Every time you take a drink of alcohol, you evaporate the lubrication lining in your throat. As alcohol flows through the blood stream, the body's water supply evaporates, thus dehydrating the body. Your body has no use for alcohol. Your liver and kidneys will work overtime to cleanse and flush alcohol from your system. This equals more trips to the bathroom. Although alcoholic drinks do contain some water, the water content isn't enough to replenish the body's evaporated supply. This is why the more you drink, the thirstier you become.

Another downfall to alcohol consumption is that the motor senses are affected. Your speech becomes slurred, your equilibrium becomes unbalanced, and your entire body becomes too relaxed to perform physical activities. Enunciation is a very important part of singing. Slurred words aren't pleasing during a song. The vocal muscles must retain a certain amount of tension to work properly. If you are too relaxed from drinking, you will lose control of your voice. If you must drink, keep it to a minimum. Plenty of water and mist inhaling is a must.

I personally don't believe the "drink one drink for relaxation" mentality. There are better ways to deal with nervousness. But, if this is your process, do what works for you.

CAFFEINE

Another dehydrator is caffeine. Caffeine is a diuretic-it will cause you to pee and lose water. Like alcohol, caffeine affects the kidneys. When the body becomes dehydrated, your vocal cords are the first to suffer. Caffeine speeds up the heart rate, agitates the nervous system, and increases your stress level. Caffeine is the only additive that mimics the effects of emotional stress. The body loses Calcium and vitamin C when under stress. Both nutrients are important for cold prevention. Stress hampers voice control. When your voice is unsteady, the quality of your sound will suffer.

Your vocal cords are coated with thin watery mucus for lubrication. Since caffeine is a diuretic it is going to pull water away from the vocal cords first. When this happens, the glands that produce mucus will continue the process, but, without enough water to dilute the consistency, your cords will be coated with thick yellow mucus that will inhibit and dampen proper vocal cord vibration. You'll notice that when you drink caffeine products, you start to clear your throat. This is an unconscious act to rid the cords of that thick yellow mucus. If you clear your throat or cough in a loud harsh manner, you will irritate the vocal cords and cause them to swell. I'm not telling you to quit, but if you do, your voice will improve.

*While on caffeine, my voice was very scratchy. But, with bold determination, (and inspiration from **Jim Gillette**), I was able to quit. The tone of my voice improved dramatically. Within two weeks, the scratchiness left, I quit clearing my throat, and my tone became clear.*

Caffeine withdrawal can cause headaches, which makes quitting difficult, but if you are determined, you can accomplish anything.

Useful Tip: Avoiding the Caffeine Cough-
If you consume a LOT of caffeine, you'll notice that you are always coughing or clearing your throat. Try to clear your throat at a low volume, suck on your lower lip, or better yet, don't clear your throat or cough at all. Your body is attempting to eliminate the yellow mucus buildup (which occurs when mucus is produced with the absence of water) from the vocal cords. If you'd drink more water, as opposed to caffeine products, this wouldn't be a problem.

COCAINE

Snorting and smoking cocaine aggravates the lining of the sinus cavity. When the mucus membranes are irritated, the sinuses produce extra mucus to flush away the irritant. Cocaine produces a numbing effect. As the affected mucus enters the throat cavity through the back of the sinuses, the throat becomes numb. This irritates the vocal cords as well, causing them to swell. When the vocal cords are swollen, they will not vibrate properly. If you attempt to sing in this state, you will endanger your voice. If you sing without physical sensation you won't be able to tell if you are straining, thus further damaging your swollen cords. The affects of cocaine stay with the voice for several days. Indulging in illegal substances for pleasure isn't worth the risk of permanently losing your voice, or getting arrested…because it is against the law!

DAIRY PRODUCTS

I love dairy products, but, when I have a vocal performance coming up, I try to eliminate them from my diet for the day of the gig. Although it doesn't seem to affect my voice much, dairy products can increase the thick mucus buildup in the body, especially in the throat. Mucus on the vocal cords hampers their ability to vibrate. Your tone will become unclear and you'll end up clearing your throat. Clearing your throat is as bad as coughing. Taking care of your voice requires commitment and sacrifice. Everyone is different, so, if dairy products affect you, I'd advise cutting back on your dairy intake before any vocal performances.

Dairy products have never been a real problem for me. Each person is different.

OVER THE COUNTER REMEDIES

Over the counter remedies include throat lozenges, throat sprays, sinus medication, and cold remedies. Although there are several good lozenges on the market, I have found few to suit me. The majority of cold products dry out the mucous linings of the throat and sinuses. Many ingredients limit the secretion of the body's natural lubricants in an attempt to mask symptoms such as coughing and congestion.

Throat lozenges do not coat the cords, only the esophagus. But the vocal cords can still be affected. Antiseptics and menthol related products dry out the throat and sinuses. Although these ingredients might open your sinus passages and numb your throat, relieving pain and congestion, the results are only temporary. Any product that dries you out is bad news. You'll have to increase your water intake in order to re-hydrate the voice.

Throat sprays are lozenges in liquid form. It is much easier to coat your throat with a spray than a lozenge. Most sprays contain similar ingredients to lozenges, with alcohol as a base. Alcohol is a drying agent. If you are using an alcohol- based spray, you are drying out your throat with each use.

Sinus medications dry out the sinus passages in an attempt to stop and break up mucus flow. Stopping mucus production sets up a home in the sinuses for bacteria to breed. Increased sinus drainage is an attempt by the body to rid itself of foreign particles in the sinuses. If the sinus passages are dried out and mucus flow is inhibited, you are not permitting the body to clean itself.

Sinus inhalers and sprays are a pitfall. They can be addictive. If you continually use nasal decongestant sprays, you risk the chance of developing *recurrent congestion*. Your sinuses will start to view the sprays as an irritant and secrete more mucus, thus adding to your congestion.

Cold remedies are similar to sinus medications. They dehydrate the body to mask the effects of a cold, preventing the body from cleaning house. Some cold remedies contain mild sedatives as a nighttime sleeping aid. In order for the body to cleanse and heal itself, it needs plenty of rest. Sedatives interrupt the body's natural sleep patterns. There are different levels of sleep that your body must cycle through several times during sleep in order for the body to revive and restore itself to a healthy state. When you are not fully refreshed, you weaken your immune system and invite infection.

If you feel that you need instant relief from a cold, don't let me sway you. I'm not condemning over-the-counter remedies, I just want to make you aware of the side effects from a singer's point of view. Any of these products can be temporarily beneficial in moderation. The choice is up to you.

SMOKING

As you well know, your vocal cords must maintain their lubrication in order to vibrate properly. **INHALING SMOKE DRIES OUT YOUR VOCAL CORDS!** Yes, I meant to shout. This refers to tobacco, marijuana, and any other substance that can be inhaled as smoke. Whether inhaling, or breathing in second hand smoke, both are harmful. In fact, second hand smoke is considered worse for your lungs because the smoke is unfiltered. Not only does smoke dry out the natural lubrication of the vocal cords, but smoke also damages the cilia. Cilia act like tiny filters, helping to prevent foreign particles and mucus from entering the lungs. Many smokers cough because the cilia are so damaged that they are unable to prevent mucus and unwanted particles from entering the lungs. As you well know, coughing is damaging to the cords.

Do yourself a favor, if you don't smoke, don't start. If you must smoke, increase your water intake to help cleanse the body. Breathing steam and mist inhaling helps to revitalize the vocal cords. Smoking depletes the body's supply of vitamin C, so taking vitamin C daily is extremely important. The best thing you can do is quit smoking. Nicotine is addictive, but if you have the desire to quit, you can beat the nicotine habit. Again your voice will thank you.

14 The Singer's Medicine Chest

I have found the following vitamins, minerals, herbs, and products to be very beneficial to maintaining a healthy voice and maintaining vocal health. There is a much wider variety than listed in this chapter, but I have chosen only to list what I have personally found beneficial to my voice. There are many detailed books on herbs and nutrition written by professionals. I am not an expert in this area. I urge you to consult your physician before taking anything in this section.

Try the following products to decide which benefit you and your body. Remember, a healthier body means a healthier voice.

APPLE CIDER VINEGAR

Apple cider vinegar boosts the immune system, purifies the cells of the body, and acts as a natural antibiotic. It is rich in vitamins, minerals, and amino acids. It improves circulation, boosts metabolism, and maintains the body's pH levels. Apple cider vinegar resembles the gastric juices, which proves beneficial in aiding digestion. It helps to flush the kidneys and liver of toxins, reduces cholesterol, and promotes weight loss. When used as a gargle, apple cider vinegar will heal a sore throat by killing the viruses and bacteria that cause a sore throat. A tablespoon of apple cider vinegar a day will keep the doctor a way.

BEE HONEY AND PROPOLIS

Both honey and bee propolis are naturally antiseptic, antibiotic, anti-fungal, and antibacterial. Propolis may also be used as an anti-inflammatory. Taken internally, propolis helps to reduce swelling of the vocal cords. It is also useful in healing wounds. The antibacterial substances in honey will help to soothe laryngitis and coughs, making it a great natural cough syrup. Several tablespoons of honey will coat and soothe the pharynx.

LEMON JUICE

Lemon juice has its pros and cons. It is beneficial to a singer when used in moderation. Lemon juice will increase saliva production, which aids dry throat, but it also contains citric acid, which is harsh on the vocal cords.

I was once told by a vocal teacher to suck on lemons and drink pure lemon juice to help my voice. For a while, while performing, I would keep lemon juice with me to drink on-stage, in between songs. Within a few short weeks I realized that this only worsened my problems. Every night during the first set, I would sound great. As the night progressed, my throat would dry out, so I would drink more lemon juice. My throat would become scratchy, and by the end of the night I could barely talk, let alone sing. Of course some of this was due to poor vocal technique, but after I quit drinking lemon juice, I quit losing my voice.

A small amount of lemon juice is beneficial, because it will cause you to salivate and help to clean out mucus from the throat. Just learn your limits with lemon juice. Again, using too much lemon juice is taxing on the cords due to the citric acid. If you feel a little dry and want to get your juices flowing, try a diluted mixture of one teaspoon of lemon juice to eight ounces of water. You will enjoy the benefits for a couple of hours.

TEA TREE OIL

Tea tree oil is a natural disinfectant and has been used for years in the medical and dental professions as an effective germicide, disinfectant and fungicide. It has also been used as a local anesthetic to relieve pain. It contains 48 organic substances that combine to establish strong healing properties. As far as a singer is concerned, tea tree oil aids in the relief of bronchitis, canker sores, colds, cold sores, laryngitis, mouth ulcers, and sinus headaches. Ten to fifteen drops in a cup of water makes an effective gargle for easing a sore throat and preventing infection.

VITAMINS AND MINERALS

Vitamins and minerals are necessary for healthy tissue growth and repair. The following vitamins and minerals aid the body in promoting a healthy voice

CALCIUM/MAGNESIUM

A supplement combination of Calcium and Magnesium help to maintain over-all health. There is more Calcium in the body than any other mineral, but you lose Calcium rapidly under stress. Calcium depletion can result in a viral infection, so a daily dose of calcium is a must for cold prevention. Magnesium enhances the absorption of Calcium in the body, reduces constriction of the bronchial tubes and strengthens the respiratory muscles. Calcium helps prevent arthritis and osteoporosis. The R.D.A. for Calcium is 1000 milligrams and 400 milligrams for Magnesium.

POTASSIUM

Potassium is the body's main healing mineral. When combined with Sodium, the body's pH levels are maintained. When this balance is upset, infection occurs. This mineral fights bacteria and viruses and flushes wastes from the body. Potassium is lost through sweating. When the body's Potassium levels are low, muscle cramping and dizziness can occur. The R.D.A. for Potassium is 3500 milligrams.

SODIUM

Sodium, or salt as it is more commonly known, is the best mineral for breaking up and flushing away excess mucus. When used as a solution for gargling or a sinus flush, salt will clean and flush bacteria infested areas. If you develop a sore throat, mix a teaspoon of salt in a cup of warm water for a gargle solution. Gargling salt water will speed the healing process.

VITAMIN B COMPLEX

Taking vitamin B Complex helps to maintain a healthy nervous system and fights mental stress and depression. Less mental stress means less tension in the throat area. When your throat is tense it is harder to sing in the upper range. B complex also relieves mouth and canker sores. The R.D.A. for vitamin B6 is two milligrams and six micrograms for B12 although you may take up to as much as 50 times the daily value. *Taking B vitamins will turn your urine bright yellow so don't be thrown into thinking that the body is dehydrated.*

VITAMIN C

Vitamin C is the singer's vitamin. It increases white blood cell count, which increases your ability to destroy viruses and bacteria, thus preventing infection. Vitamin C is a natural antihistamine, which is beneficial to sinus sufferers. If your body's vitamin C reserve is depleted, infection can spread. If you are a smoker, you have a greater risk of catching a cold. Tobacco breaks down vitamin C in the body. You also lose vitamin C when you are under mental stress. Stress can lead to exhaustion and sickness. The Recommended Daily Allowance is 60 milligrams; however, vitamin C is not toxic in large quantities. During cold season, your body could require as much as 2000 milligrams, three to four times daily. Massive doses can cause diarrhea.

ZINC

If vitamin C is the singer's vitamin, then Zinc is the singer's mineral. It is an important mineral for resisting infection in the body. If Zinc is taken in the form of a lozenge, it will help to relieve a sore throat as well as reduce inflammation of the vocal cords. Taking Zinc tabs during a performance can help to maintain your singing voice. Zinc deficiency shows up in the form of white spots on the fingernails. Add Zinc to your daily regimen to reduce the risk of catching a cold. The R.D.A. is 12 milligrams for women and 15 milligrams for men. In order to relieve a sore throat, twice the amount might be required.
HIGH DOSAGES OF ZINC OVER A LONG PERIOD OF TIME CAN BE TOXIC, AFFECTING PROPER IMMUNE SYSTEM FUNCTION.

Useful Tip: Liquid Form is Better-

*It is better to take your vitamins and minerals in liquid form. Liquid form is absorbed into the blood stream faster than pill form. You may not be getting the full benefit from pill form, because a pill is not always fully digested. Not to be gross, but an owner of a portable toilet company said that when the toilets are cleaned, he has seen tons of pills that said "One-A-Day" on them. So go to your local **GNC** and check out the liquid vitamin and mineral section.*

HERBS

Herbs serve as preventive maintenance for colds. The following list of herbs benefit the voice.

Chamomile- Fights colds, coughs, and congestion. A natural sleep inducer.

Chlorophyll- Two tablespoons of liquid chlorophyll will detoxify germs that cause a sore throat and help eliminate bad breath.

Collinsonia- Relieves laryngitis and throat irritation.

Echinacea- Natural antibiotic. This herb helps to clean the lymphatic system and flushes toxins out of the body. Increases the production of white blood cells and slows down the spreading of bacteria and viral infections in the body. Stimulates the immune system. Fights sinus infections, tonsillitis, and laryngitis.

Ginseng- An excellent herb for fighting physical and emotional stress. Ginseng increases energy and stamina. Replenishes the body's energy levels when you are tired.

Goldenseal - Another natural antibiotic. Flushes toxins from the body. Reduces inflammation of the mucus membranes of the sinuses and throat. Relieves sore throat, tonsillitis, sinusitis, and allergies.

Kelp- AKA seaweed, is a natural source of iodine, which is beneficial for proper thyroid functioning. Kelp contains over 70 vitamins, minerals, trace elements, and enzymes. When taken with meals, kelp aids digestion.

Licorice- A natural form of cortisone, which can reduce the swelling of inflamed vocal cords. Replenishes the body's energy by feeding the adrenal glands. Rebuilds the tissue and mucus membranes of the sinuses and throat. Licorice is a natural antihistamine.

Lobelia- Powerful lung cleanser. Breaks up and flushes excessive mucus from the body. **LOBELIA IS TOXIC IN LARGE DOSES.**

Mullein- Relieves sinus congestion, sore throat, coughs, and bronchitis.

Osha Root- Natural lung cleanser. Loosens mucus buildup.

Slippery Elm- The best herb for soothing a sore throat. Slippery Elm lubricates the throat and reduces inflammation of the throat and vocal cords. Best taken as a throat lozenge or herbal tea.

St. John's Wort- Natural mood elevator. Helps to fight depression and mental stress.

Useful Tip: Health Handbook-
*The **Health Handbook** by **Louise Tenny** is an excellent resource for ailments and a listing of the best vitamins, minerals, nutritional supplements, herbs, and herbal combinations to alleviate each ailment and cleanse the body of infection.*

Useful Tip: Do a Little Research-
The vitamins and minerals that I have listed are not the only choices for vocal health. There are all sorts of information on vitamins and minerals, and a multitude of other health related supplements that will benefit your over-all heath, as well as your singing voice. Do yourself a favor and do a little research of your own to find other sources.

Useful Tip: Reflexology For Singers-

*Reflexology is another field that I consider to be of great importance to vocal health. Reflexology is a science that corresponds to reflex areas in the feet and hands that are related to all of the glands, organs, and parts of the body. I believe that a sore throat can be relieved by reflexology. There is an interesting story about a famous concert singer regaining her upper register with the aid of reflexology in the book, **Better Health With Foot Reflexology,** by **Dwight C. Byers.***

A simple massage routine for singers begins by squeezing and releasing the tips of all fingers and toes, seven times each. Then massage each finger and toe, all the way around each digit. If you find any soreness, stop and massage that area until the soreness is gone. The fingers and toes all relate to the head and sinuses.

Next, massage around the base of the thumbs and big toes, and the web between the thumb and forefinger, as well as the web between the big toe and second toe. This area is related to the throat, neck, and thyroid.

Then, massage the top and bottom of the wrist. This area is related to the lymphatic system, which is the body's garbage collector. This improves lymphatic drainage.

Finally, massage across the top of the hand within two inches of the knuckles and the bottom of the foot, within two inches of the pads of the toes. This area is related to the lungs a diaphragm.

Although this basic routine is beneficial for singers when combating vocal ailments, I'd suggest adopting this routine every day. Don't forget to research reflexology to develop a more advanced routine.

15 The Singer's Daily Regimen

The cells of your body rely on vitamins and minerals to maintain health and to reproduce. The average person does not receive the proper nutrition from daily meals. You may be filling your stomach but starving your cells. It is important to add a **multiple vitamin** and **mineral complex** to your daily regimen. Consider using liquid vitamins and colloidal minerals. Both allow full absorption into the blood stream. **Vitamin C** and **Calcium** break down easily from stress, so you should add these individual nutrients as well. **Zinc** is the singer's mineral, and should be added. It helps to rebuild throat tissue and will relieve a sore throat. **Vitamin B Complex** should be added to relieve stress. Although multiple vitamins contain the previous, it is to your benefit to add them individually. Add a supplement reference book to your bookshelf so you can check daily allowances for the vitamins and minerals mentioned. Check out *Earl Mindell's Vitamin* and *Herb Bibles*.

An herbal combination of **Goldenseal** and **Echinacea** helps to fight infection in the body. Please note that a continual daily use of this combination will develop a tolerance in the body within two to three months. I recommend taking it daily only during a cold and once or twice a week during healthy times. When taking this combination, add **Bee Propolis** to act as an internal disinfectant, aiding the body's house cleaning duties. **Colloidal Silver** is the only known substance that can kill over 650 different types of viruses and bacteria. It isn't toxic and can be taken internally. Your body will not develop a tolerance from **colloidal silver** so you might want to use it daily for mist inhaling. This will help to heal a sore throat. **Ginseng** is a natural energy booster that will keep you going throughout your daily routine. A tablespoon of **liquid chlorophyll** a day will keep a sore throat away. **Apple cider vinegar tea** is a must. One tablespoon of apple cider vinegar and one tablespoon of honey in a cup of water will maintain the body's pH balance, aid digestion, and fight infection.

Useful Tip: Make Your Own Colloidal Silver-

There is a website called Sunstone Herbals, __http://www.sunstoneherbals.com,__ that sells a small device called a colloidal silver generator. You can make gallons of colloidal silver for pennies a day within minutes. I own one and use it every day.

Useful Tip: Your Diet-

If you are really serious about vocal health, you might consider taking a look at your diet. Avoid refined sugar and flour, caffeine, and fat. Increase your intake of whole grains, fruits & vegetables, and protein sources such as chicken and fish. Purchase a few books that explain the dieting process. Being a singer, again I suggest focusing on vegetables, fruits, and low-fat protein sources.

Useful Tip: I Need Sugar!

Yes, you do need sugar-natural sugar is a necessary part of your diet, but that doesn't mean you need a candy bar. Processed sugar will actually deplete important vitamins from your system, and requires lots of energy to digest. The rush of energy you feel from a chocolate chip cookie is because of the sudden release of insulin as a result of sugar. This is why people will have a chocolate bar when they feel weak- in order to release insulin into their bloodstream for a quick energy pick-me up. But processed sugar takes more energy to digest than is initially released. If you need a quick boost of energy, try a natural source of sugar, like apples, oranges, or bananas. Natural sources of sugar will not strip the body of vitamins. Apple juice is a great pick me up beverage for that little boost of energy.

Useful Tip: Never Get Another Cold!

*If you are REALLY serious about changing your diet, I suggest purchasing "**Never Get Another Cold**", by vocal coach **Thomas Appell. Thomas,** (also the author of **"Can You Sing A High C Without Straining?"**) has created a revolutionary diet that will restore your health and eliminate the common cold.*

The previous daily dose is from my personal daily ritual and what I have found necessary to help keep my vocal instrument in perfect condition. The following list of items, (although not a daily requirement), are items that I have found to be beneficial to my voice:

ENTERTAINER'S SECRET THROAT SPRAY

Entertainer's Secret Throat Relief is a spray formulated to resemble the natural mucus secretions and designed to moisturize, humidify, and lubricate the mucus membranes of the throat and larynx. This spray supplements the throat's natural lubricants. It contains **Aloe Vera gel, glycerin, and Sodium Carboxycellulose**, all which closely resemble the body's natural lubricating substances. Unlike other throat sprays, this spray does not contain alcohol, antiseptics, analgesics, antihistamines, decongestants, or anti-inflammatory agents.

When mist inhaled, it coats, soothes, and re-lubricates the vocal cords. It can also be directly inhaled into the nose to relieve sinus congestion and lubricate dry sinus passages. Except for pure water, this is the only spray I recommend using. It's like lotion for the skin, only for the vocal cords.

THROAT LOZENGES

For years, vocalists have used throat lozenges to soothe a sore throat. When choosing a lozenge, stay away from any that contain alcohol, menthol, antihistamines, antiseptics, or decongestants. Look for lozenges that contain supplements that are beneficial to the voice. **Slippery Elm** lozenges are top of the list for coating and lubricating the pharynx. Lozenges containing **Vitamin C** and **Zinc** boost the immune system and relieve sore throat pain. **Chewable Papaya tablets** are excellent for relieving sinus congestion. Lozenges containing **honey** and **glycerin** coat and lubricate the throat. **Licorice** is natural cortisone and will reduce swelling. **Apple pectin** has been proven to ease a sore throat. If you find a lozenge that contains all of the above, please let me know.

THROAT COAT TEA

One tea that I consider food for voice is an herbal tea called **Throat Coat** by **Traditional Medicinals**. This tea contains no caffeine, which as you know, is bad for the voice. The main ingredients are **slippery elm bark** and **licorice root**. Both **licorice root** and **slippery elm** helps to soothe, moisturize and reduce the swelling of the vocal cords. I recommend a cup a day.

FIXER ELIXIR

A fixer elixir is a combination of ingredients that can be used as a gargle solution to relieve sore throat pain. The following list of ingredients can be used individually or in combination with one cup of warm water:

1. **Apple Cider Vinegar**- One tablespoon- Kills bacteria in the throat.
2. **Aloe Vera Juice**- Two tablespoons- Lubricates throat.
3. **Capsicum**- One opened capsule or pinch of pepper- Improves circulation in throat.
4. **Glycerin**- Five to ten drops- Lubricates throat.
5. **Honey**- Two tablespoons- Coats throat.
6. **Lemon Juice**- One teaspoon- Increases saliva production.
7. **Liquid Chlorophyll**- One tablespoon- Acts as healing agent.
8. **Salt**- One teaspoon- breaks up congestion, flushes mucus.
9. **Tea Tree Oil**- Five to ten drops- a natural disinfectant.
10. **Peroxide**- One teaspoon- Kills bacteria in throat.
11. **Licorice**-5-10 drops of liquid licorice-Reduces swelling.
12. **Colloidal silver**-Can be used as a base in place of water.

With twelve ingredients from which to choose, there are numerous possible combinations. I urge you to try as many combinations as needed until you find one that suits you. The amount suggested for each ingredient is general. Once you develop your magical elixir combination, you can adjust the amount of each ingredient to fit your needs.

Four of the ingredients listed can be used independently at full strength-A-3% **hydrogen peroxide** solution, **colloidal silver, liquid chlorophyll,** or **Tea Tree Oil** can be used as a mouthwash or gargle. Both **liquid chlorophyll** and **colloidal silver** are better when ingested.

It is best to use warm water when mixing a gargle solution. This can be either room temperature or hot water. Make sure that it isn't too hot, or you'll burn your throat and the heat will cause the vocal cords to swell. Gargle the solution three to five times. **Do not gargle with laryngitis**. Only gargle to relieve a sore throat or congestion. Don't feel limited to the twelve ingredients mentioned. Do some research to find other ingredients that suit your needs.

Useful Tip: Making Your Own Tea-

*You can also use several of these ingredients for making a tea-like drink. You can use any ingredient you choose, except for peroxide or tea tree oil. These two ingredients are not meant to be ingested. **James Labrie** drinks hot water and honey when performing and warming up. He keeps two thermoses on stage-one out front with the band, and one back stage, to sip from during solos.*

ORAL HYGIENE

An area much overlooked as applied to singing is oral hygiene. In order to help keep bacteria to a minimum, you need to brush and floss your teeth two to three times daily. There are several types of toothpaste from which to choose. If you prefer something simpler, a combination of salt and baking soda acts as a tooth polish. Salt cleans and hardens the teeth, and baking soda acts as a mild polish to prevent plaque buildup. Another home for bacteria is the tongue. Brushing the tongue will remove some bacteria but the best way to clean the tongue is to use a tongue scraper. You can purchase a tongue scraper from any pharmacy or health food store.

Useful Tip: Serious Oral Care-

*If you have ever thought about using an electric toothbrush, **Sonic1** is the choice for you. **Sonic1** is a new electric toothbrush from the makers of **Cybersonic**. **Sonic1** operates like a tuning fork, at 47,000 strokes per minute. The inventor, **Dr. Ron Murayama**, sent me one of his new inventions to try for myself. I was amazed at how clean my teeth felt after my first time using the **Sonic1** toothbrush. It felt like I had just had my teeth professionally cleaned at my dentist office. After using the brush for a few days, I threw out my old manual brush and will always use my **Sonic1**. Other benefits are the flossing and tongue scraping attachments, and the teeth bleaching system. If oral care is important to you, as it should be, you should check out the **Sonic1** toothbrush.*

To kill bacteria in the back of the throat and tonsils, I advise using a mouthwash. Food can get lodged behind the tonsils, providing a home for bacteria to breed. Gargling will help release any food caught in the back of the throat. Peroxide is my mouthwash of choice. It will kill bacteria without drying out the throat. Tea Tree Oil is another excellent mouthwash as well. You can also spray colloidal silver into the back of the throat to kill bacteria. Any alcohol- based mouthwash will dry out the throat. Your goal should be to practice oral hygiene regardless of your choice of toothpaste or mouthwash.

Useful Tip: A Health Tip Before A Performance-

There are two supplements that I always use before a performance-zinc and licorice. I take two 23-milligram zinc (chewable) tablets and one capsule of licorice, about thirty minutes prior to hitting the stage. Zinc rebuilds and strengthens throat tissue and licorice reduces vocal cord swelling, both of which are beneficial to vocal health.

Useful Tip: Preventative Maintenance-

*If you truly want to stay healthy, you should follow some sort of preventative maintenance program. Although I have presented you with a "Singer's Daily Dose", each person is unique and must discover what combination of nutrients best serves them, as an individual. The "Daily Dose" is the program that I follow for my vocal health. Regardless of what you choose, if you do not follow your daily regimen, you are at higher risk of catching a cold or some type of infection. I realized this recently when I caught a sinus and chest infection. I was extremely worn down from rewriting this book, filming an infomercial, filming various video clips, including a video for **Guinness World Records**, and working on updates for **The Voice Connection**. I had not been taking my daily dose, or my allergy shots, and became susceptible to a cold. If you find yourself under stress, and tired from lack of sleep, DO NOT forget your daily regimen, or the flu bug just might bite! (Don't forget to check out "**Never Get Another Cold**" by **Thomas Appell**.)*

Part Three Raising The Voice

Vocal health is an important part of developing your voice. If a machine isn't maintained then how can you expect it to function properly? You are a machine, so if you wish to become a great singer, then you must be properly maintained. Now that you've acquired vocal knowledge and health, it is time to develop vocal technique. Let's RAISE YOUR VOICE!

The following exercises are the greatest tools I have found for strengthening the voice. They will not only extend the range, increase the power, and improve the quality of your voice, but also help keep the voice in excellent health. The best thing about this program is that you can perform the exercises anytime and anywhere. All you need to perform the routine is a pitch wheel, drinking water, a mist bottle, and a mirror if you wish to check for facial stress.

There are several rules to be followed when performing these exercises:

1. **Keep the vocal cords lubricated**. This means plenty of drinking water, as well as gargling and mist inhaling during practice. Don't forget to breathe in through your nose. The cords dry out easily due to excessive vocalizing.

2. You must make sure that you use **breath control** and have mastered your **breath technique**. If you do not apply proper breath technique during practice and performance, your voice will tire and strain. Focus on the **inhalation sensation**.

3. **Do not rush these exercises**. Take your time. The slower you perform them, the more control you will have over vocal cord positioning. This will help to eliminate any wavering or breaking up of the voice.

4. **Correct posture** allows the voice to flow freely. Slouching interrupts the natural path of the **core of resonance**. The path should be a straight line from the diaphragm to the top of the head. Poor posture throws the spine out of alignment. When the spine is misaligned, the imbalance creates muscle tension, stressing the vocal cords.

5. **If you suspect unnecessary muscle tension, perform the** *muscle stress check.* As you sing or perform a vocal exercise, slowly move your head side to side as if you are shaking your head *"no."* If the pitch disconnects and breaks up, you are tensing the cords too tightly. Try relaxing the throat, stomach muscles to back off the breath support. When the pitch becomes steady, you have established the proper amount of breath support and vocal cord tension required for proper **zipper technique**. Use this technique any time during practice when you start feeling uncomfortable.

6. **If the muscles under your chin become sore, stop and rest for a minute.** This is a good thing. You are strengthening the muscles that control larynx positioning and help to control vocal cord adjustment. This is just like working out with weights; you take a break in between sets to allow the muscles to relax for a moment. Resting your voice for a moment or two will result in quicker vocal development. However, if the muscles under your chin stay sore, check to see if these muscles are tight as you sing. They should stay relaxed as if you were yawning. When you yawn, the chin muscles drop down, but do not tighten. If at any time these muscles become tight, stop the exercise. Try maintaining a yawn position to prevent this from happening.

7. **Always aim for a clean tone.** When performing full voice exercises, aim for a clean resonant tone. Feel the resonance in your chest on low notes, in your throat on mid-notes, and in your head on high notes. If you get dizzy on high notes, congratulations. You are really resonating the cathedral inside of your head. Even though you imagine breathing in your sound, this resonant tone must physically leave your body. Try to feel the sensation of your teeth buzzing as you sing. **The sensation of buzzing teeth proves that you are producing plenty of resonance.** Remember, the more resonance you produce, the easier it will be to sing any pitch.

DISCLAIMER: The following sections are not intended to prevent or treat any physical conditions. Before performing any of the following exercises, I urge you to consult your physician.

16 Vocal Stress Release

Throughout the day, our bodies absorb a great amount of physical stress. Symptoms of stress include aching feet, stiff back, and headaches. Stress affects your voice, limiting your ability to sing open and freely. To reach and maximize your voice potential, you must release any stress that could inhibit the vocal process. The following series of exercises release muscle tension and prepare the voice for singing.

The **Vocal Stress Release Program** is a warm up system that I designed to minimize physical stress and create a positive physical state, to enhance vocal production. The **Vocal Stress Release Program** should be performed before any vocal exercises are conducted. In addition, this program may be performed at any time to relieve stress. The following series of stretches and exercises should be conducted in the order in which they are presented in this chapter:

THE VOCAL STRESS RELEASE PROGRAM

DEEP BREATHING

This exercise helps to calm the mind and body. Deep breathing will focus your center of concentration, a practice that is invaluable for singing. Deep breathing stretches and relaxes the chest cavity, back muscles, and diaphragm, all of which are used for vocal control.

1. Inhale through your nose to a count of eight, filling the lungs from the bottom up.

    a. First, your waist should expand all the way around your body.

    b. Next, your sides, back muscles and lower ribs will expand.

    c. Last, your upper chest should expand.

    d. This completes one full inhale.

2. Hold your breath to a count of four.

    a. When you hold your breath, don't lock the breath or grunt.

    b. Pretend as if you are still inhaling. (**Inhalation sensation**)

3.   Next, exhale through your mouth to a count of sixteen.

a. Empty your lungs as much as possible, ridding the lungs of any stale air. When exhaling, hiss the air out. This will tighten the stomach and back causing the muscles to ache. Don't worry, this is not adding stress, but strengthening the muscles used for breath control.

b. Try to prevent your stomach from falling in. Keep it expanded.

c. Controlled air release will strengthen your diaphragm.

Do not skip this exercise. Deep breathing relaxes the body and serves as the basis for breath support, which is important for singing long phrases. Repeat the entire breathing process five to ten times. **Deep Breathing Example**

NECK TENSION RELEASE

This exercise stretches out the neck muscles and releases tension.

1. **SIDE TO SIDE:**

a. Take your left hand and place it on the right side of your head, with your fingers pointed down towards your shoulders.

b. Gently pull the right side of your head towards your left shoulder. You should feel a pull in the right side of your neck. **Do not pull beyond the point of pain!** You only want to feel the stretch in your neck. Hold to a count of ten.

c.   As you count, continue pulling your neck towards your shoulder with your hand. This will stretch out the neck muscles, making them more limber.

d. Repeat this process using your right hand to pull the left side of your head. After a few weeks, you can increase the count to twenty or more, for a deeper stretch.

2. **BACK AND FORTH:**

a. Allow your head to fall backwards until you are looking up at the ceiling.

b. Put your hands underneath your chin and gently push your head backward to stretch out the area of the larynx.

c. Hold to a count of ten.

d. Next, drop your head forward toward the ground.

e. Take both of your hands and place them on the back of your head and pull your head down, bringing your chin to your chest.

> ***f.*** Use both of your hands to pull your head deeper into your chest until you can feel the muscles in the back of your neck stretching. As I said before, **do not force beyond the point of pain**.
>
> ***g.*** Hold to a count of ten, maintaining constant pressure from your hands to enhance the stretch. After a period of time you can increase your hold count.

3. **NECK ROLLS:**
   - ***a.*** Start with your head hanging forward.
   - ***b.*** Roll your head to the right. Your shoulders will want to move as you roll. If you notice this happening, concentrate on keeping them still and straight. Allowing your shoulders to roll with your head will not permit your neck to fully relax and release tension.
   - ***c.*** When performing this exercise, allow your head to hang as far forward towards the floor as possible, as if gravity was pulling your head to the floor regardless of head position (forwards, backwards or to the sides).
   - ***d.*** Continue to roll your head slowly around your right side, then to the back.
   - ***e.*** When you reach this point, your head should be all the way back. You should be able to see the ceiling.
   - ***f.*** Continue rolling your head to your left side, and finally back to the front.
   - ***g.*** Repeat the process ten times to the right, then ten times to the left. By the time the neck exercises are done, your neck should feel pretty loose and relaxed.

   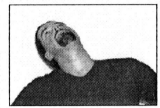

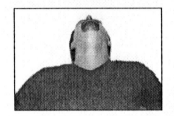 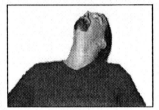 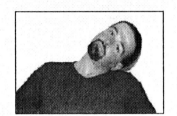 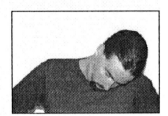

4. **NECK MUSCLE MASSAGE:** Massaging the neck relieves tension in the neck and throat area.

   a. Start by massaging the back of your neck. Use both hands to squeeze and release the muscles, loosening any knots or kinks.

   b. Then take your thumbs and work them into your neck muscles in a circular motion until you have done this over the entire back of your neck.

   c. Work your thumbs up to where the neck meets the skull, then down until your neck meets the back of your shoulders.

   d. After the back of the neck is complete, continue on to the sides of the neck. Use the same massage process for the sides, as you did for the back of the neck. Use the left hand for the left side, and use the right hand for the right side.

   e. After you feel that you have thoroughly massaged the sides, take all of your fingers and, starting at the bottom of the sides of your neck, slowly rub upwards until you reach the protruding part of the skull, right behind your ears, on the sides of your head.

5. **THROAT MUSCLE MASSAGE:** The front of the neck requires a different massage process.

   a. Start at the collarbone and work the fingers of both hands down into the indentures of the collarbone.

b. Start on the outer sides and work towards the middle. Work your fingers in a slow circular motion being careful not to cause any discomfort.
c. When both sides are complete, place the middle and index finger of your hands into the indenture in the center of your collarbone and massage in a circular motion. Massage the front of your throat as you did the sides of the neck.
  e. After the front of the neck is completely massaged, move on to the muscles under the chin.

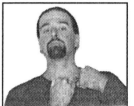

6. **CHIN MASSAGE:** The muscles under the chin play an important role in singing, helping to maintain a low larynx position and an open vocal path. This area can hold a lot of tension. Use both hands for this massage technique

a. Place your fingers up under your chin.
b. Massage the chin muscles by working your fingers in a circular motion, starting underneath your jawbones.
c. Massage the entire area of the muscle, working your fingers towards your chin.
  d. Next, squeeze and release the muscles under the chin to loosen any knotted muscles.

FACIAL TENSION RELEASE

1. **JAW TENSION RELEASE:** If you clinch or grind your teeth, you will carry tension in your jaws, making it difficult to sing openly and enunciate words clearly.

a. Start by pressing the fingers of each hand into the indenture in front of your ears.
b. Now yawn. Did you feel the indenture getting deeper in front of your ears? This is the **temporal mandibular joint**.

c. Massage the entire area, down to where the jaw line meets the neck, and up to the temples.

d. After you have massaged the temporal mandibular joint, press your fingers into the indenture and pull your jawbone towards the front of your face, stretching out the jawbone. As always, do not pull past the point of pain. Do this two-five times.

e. Lastly, use your right thumb, right side and left thumb, left side, to "pull" all remaining tension down along the jaw line to the chin. Simply use the thumbs and slide along the jawbone down to the chin bone. Do this several times until all soreness is gone.

Useful Tip: Pulling and Releasing Jaw Tension-

Another method for releasing jaw tension is by placing each thumb inside your mouth, up against the hard palate and pulling the teeth apart from each other, (like widening the hard palate). Pull the thumbs towards your cheeks (right thumb pulls to the right cheek, left thumb pulls to the left cheek). Perform this routine about three times in a row, starting at the front of the mouth and moving back tooth by tooth until you have reached the back of the mouth. This helps to release tension that has developed from gritting your teeth or clenching your mouth.

2. **CRAZY FACE**: This exercise relieves tension held in the facial muscles.

a. Start by yawning.

b. As you yawn, stretch both your mouth and eyes as wide open as you can, then stick out your tongue as far as possible.

As you stretch your tongue, it might feel a little sore. The tongue has a tendency to knot up towards the back of the throat. Stress is stored in your muscles, which produce knots and muscle spasms. The tongue is one of the strongest muscles in your body and it can hold a lot of tension.

c. Hold this facial position to a count of ten. I know this looks really funny, but it is the best way to release facial tension.

d. Now, open and close your mouth as in a big over exaggerated chewing movement. Do this several times.

e. Lastly, wiggle your jaw side to side several times. Now that you've stretched your face, let's revisit the tongue.

TONGUE TENSION RELEASE

The tongue can hold a large amount of tension, causing the back of the tongue to rise and knot up. A tense tongue will constrict the vocal path, making the opening in the back of the throat smaller. A smaller vocal path results in a smaller, pinched sound. You need a way to help stretch out the tongue and loosen the knots.

The best way to relax the tongue is by stretching. Begin by drying off your tongue with a towel or handkerchief and then use your hand to pull and stretch your tongue out of your mouth. If your hand slips, then you can also use a dry towel to hold on to your tongue while you pull. Pull down and out for a good stretch. As you pull, concentrate on relaxing your tongue, to stretch the tongue further. Do this exercise 5-10 times, or until you have released any soreness in your tongue.

Useful Tip: Pulling Out Tongue Tension From the Back to the Front-
Another way to stretch and release tension in the tongue is by "pulling out tension. Place your pointer finger on the base of the tongue in the front of your mouth and slowly slide it towards the back of the throat. Any time that you reach a knot or the tongue begins to buckle up, pause and relax that area by massaging your tongue with your finger until the tongue relaxes. Your goal is to eventually work your finger all the way back until you reach the root of the tongue, which is down in the throat. This will disengage the gag reflex and teach you to release the knots of tension in the tongue, which will train the tongue to keep from raising up in the mouth and blocking off the vocal path.

DIAPHRAGM TENSION RELEASE

Your diaphragm can slide up underneath the ribcage from the affects of poor posture (slouching). This exercise relieves tension in your diaphragm by returning the diaphragm to its proper position. The correct position is right below the ribcage. Take your hands and massage your stomach down, starting to the left or right of the ribcage. Work from the left or right of the rib cage down to the middle, where your ribs meet.

Next, bend over forward at the waist with the legs firmly planted straight. Let the body hang forward to stretch the spine. Then, with the left hand hanging loosely at you side, raise your right hand above your head, then, lean over towards your left side, pointing the hand above your head (right hand) towards the left side of the floor. This will stretch out the right side of your body and ribs. Repeat this process with your left hand in the air, and right arm dangling loosely, while stretching to the right. Finally, lift both hands above your head and lean back as far as possible (without falling over). This will stretch the diaphragm, stomach muscles and the front of the ribs.

LIP BUBBLES

Lip bubbles relax and warm up the entire vocal mechanism. Performing this exercise increases blood flow to your vocal cords and surrounding muscles, preparing your voice for a vocal workout or performance.

Lip bubbles are also known as motorboats due to the fact that the sound produced sounds much like a motorboat running in the water. This is similar to a horse pursing its lips and blowing out air. To produce this tone, purse your lips together, then force air between them. A consistent flow of air is required to vibrate your lips evenly. If you do not gain balance between your lip tension and the applied air pressure, your lips will not continue to vibrate.

When you can produce lip bubbles, apply tone to the exercise. Concentrate on the feeling of tone hitting and passing through your lips. Lip bubbles disconnect your mental connection to the vocal cords. The sound will feel as if is being produced by your lips. This is the perfect exercise for relieving vocal strain and preparing the voice for an intense vocal workout!

Starting on any note, produce lip bubbles while maintaining a consistent pitch for several seconds, then slide to the bottom of your range. **Lip Bubbles Example** Repeat this exercise 10-15 times, each time starting on a different pitch. It's best performed when starting somewhere in your lower range, then working your way up to higher pitches. When you are ready, proceed to the next step of **Vocal Stress Release.**

GARGLING TONE

Gargling tone was previously explained in **Chapter six, HYDRATING THE VOICE**. Gargling tone is perfect for warming up. It works hand in hand with lip bubbles. Lip bubbles warm up and expand the cords, much like stretching out your body. The gargling tone exercise relaxes and hydrates the voice, much like relaxing in a Jacuzzi. The same steps apply to this exercise as lip bubbles.

Start by taking a small amount of water in your mouth, then tilt your head back, and gargle on any pitch. Sustain the pitch for a few seconds, and then slide down to the bottom of your range. This takes consistent breath support and a constant stream of air to prevent from swallowing water while vocalizing. Repeat this exercise 2-3 times. **Gargling Tone Example** I usually use this exercise throughout my entire routine. Whenever I'm feeling a little dry or need a quick break, I'll gargle on tone in between exercises or songs.

RESONANCE HUM

To perform the resonance hum exercise, simply close your mouth and hum until your teeth begin to buzz. This creates resonance in the mouth cavity. You'll soon discover that you can expand this feeling of resonance to the entire head cavity. I want you to feel your cheeks, nose, teeth, and even your ears buzzing. Hum on any pitch that is comfortable for your range. **Resonance Hum Example** Sustain the pitch for as long as comfortable. Next, try humming while allowing the pitch to slide down to the bottom of your range. Don't force yourself to produce any resonance; allow it to happen naturally. This exercise massages the vocal cords and relieves tightness. Perform this exercise at least 10-15 times on different pitches.

VOCAL CORD STRETCH

The vocal cord stretch is actually a fast continual version of one of the main exercises in this book, called **THE SIREN**. Before you start performing this particular warm-up exercise as part of **Vocal Stress Release**, you must fully understand and have been practicing **THE SIREN** regularly.

To perform the vocal cord stretch, sustain a full voice pitch. Next raise the pitch up as high as comfortable, then return to the beginning pitch. Continue to raise and drop the pitch as many times as you can on one breath.

To effectively and correctly perform this exercise, the tone must be clean and extremely resonant. Remember, the voice is shaped like a triangle. As you slide up in pitch, (or ascend the scale) the tone will get thinner and pointier, and as you slide back down in pitch (descend), the tone will widen back out and become fuller. Keep the buzzing sensation on your teeth, and follow the path of your **core of resonance.** Following the path will be further explained in the following chapters. Perform this exercise 10-15 times or until your voice feels loosened up and you are ready to perform. **Vocal Cord Stretch Example**

This completes **Vocal Stress Release**. You should feel warmed up and ready for your vocal workout. The only other thing you might wish to do is to perform a few mist inhales, and drink some water before your workout or performance. Now it's time to proceed to the voice strengthening exercises.

Useful Tip: Humming Up-

*A lot of professional singers will sing songs after warming up and prior to performing. **Sahaj Ticotin** of **RA** prefers to "hum" his way to a warm voice. If you want to try this approach, pick out five or six songs, (or as many as it takes) to perform after you have finished your warm up. Begin the first couple of songs by lightly humming along with the lyrics. If the song is a high song, like **Coshise** by **Audioslave**, hum the song one octave lower in pitch, in your speaking level. When you hum the next few songs, hum on the actual pitch. For the next song, try singing the song as softly as possible (without using a whisper tone). When you reach your last song, sing it just like you would perform the song live!*

17 The Falsetto Slide

Falsetto is one of the greatest tools for extending your range. The purpose of this exercise is to develop greater flexibility and to smooth out the entire falsetto range. Working your falsetto first prepares your vocal cords for tighter, more demanding tensions. Your vocal cords still zip together but not at as tight a tension as full voice. When first developing your vocal muscles, it is easier for the cords to zip together in falsetto.

Stretch your mouth open wide and yawn. Let go of any tension. Yawn once again, but this time, vocalize as you yawn. I'm sure you've done this a hundred times before. As you yawn just say "*ah*." Start with a high, but light pitch and let the sound slide smoothly down to your lower range. Remember, when using falsetto, you want the same tone that singers like **Prince** or **Jeff Buckley** use for their upper range.

Useful Tip: Not Your Typical Falsetto-
To achieve maximum results from this exercise, you DO NOT want to sing with a typical breathy falsetto sound. Although I want you to produce the same tonal quality as Prince, I want you to create as clear a tone as possible. So, if you hear any breathiness, concentrate on cleaning up that breathy tone until the sound is very focused and pure!

You don't want to actually yawn during the exercise. Your goal is to maintain a **yawning sensation** without yawning. The **yawning sensation** lowers the larynx and creates a dome-like shape in the back of the throat by raising the soft palate and lowering the tongue to a U-shaped position. **A high palate and lowered U-shaped tongue opens the vocal path and allows the sound to flow freely up the throat and out the mouth.** Keep the tip of the tongue against the back of your bottom front teeth in order to maintain the U-shaped position. Sometimes, keeping a low larynx position can be difficult. You can touch your Adam's apple to make sure it is behaving, and if it isn't, yawn again to lower it down.

With all of the basics out of the way, grab your keyboard or pitch wheel, and start on a note that is in your lower mid-range. Men should start on Middle C, or C4, an octave below Tenor high C. Women should start five notes higher on F4. Use these same starting points for the rest of the exercises. These notes are your **points of reference** for the sake of teaching in this book. In the course of your normal practice, you might want to start higher or lower, depending on what is comfortable for your vocal range.

RAISE YOUR VOICE

There are several conditions you must meet when performing this exercise. **First,** make sure that you have taken a sufficient breath, and maintain your breath support. **Second,** visualize your **core of resonance**. This is a major key to reaching higher notes. The more focused you are upon your **core of resonance**, the easier you'll be able to sing higher notes. **Third,** sing as soft as you can with as little air as possible. By eliminating any breathiness from your falsetto you are learning to produce falsetto with minimum breath support while also protecting your throat from drying out.

Start by singing *"ah"* as in *"father"* as soft and clear as possible. The sound may have a tendency to waiver, but as you develop strength and coordination, this will pass, and the note will stay even for as long as you sustain each pitch.

As you sustain the word *"ah,"* notice how the pitch feels in your throat. Where is the majority of resonance created? If the resonance is created down low in your body, then the **core of resonance** should be low.

FALSETTO RESONANCE

Falsetto resonance is not as intense as full voice resonance. Imagine your **core of resonance** having a light glow while singing in falsetto. Your **core of resonance** is no bigger than a ping-pong ball. Keep the note as even as possible. If the **core of resonance** is hovering evenly, then your voice should flow evenly.

As you begin to run out of breath, your stomach and back muscles will start to burn. This is great. Now you are performing two exercises in one, and you didn't even know it. **Sustaining notes for long durations is the key to developing breath support for long phrases.** In the beginning, you might not be able to hold a note very long, but that's normal. As you progress, you'll hold tones for longer periods.

Don't strain at any time! If you start to strain, stop and give yourself a break. You'll have a tendency to tighten your stomach as you begin to run out of breath. Do not purposely tighten your stomach muscles. Allow your stomach to fall in naturally.

When you are almost out of breath, slide the pitch all the way down to the lowest note in your range. As the vocally slide to the bottom, imagine your **core of resonance** sliding down as well. As you slide, you will reach a point when you are not in falsetto, but you should keep the tone of your voice consistent in volume all the way down to the bottom of your range.

Your voice may break as you slide; you want to develop muscular coordination so that this does not occur. If this happens, stop, repeat the exercise, and **slide very slowly through the breaking area**. This will give your muscles time to adjust to the different pulls on your vocal cords. Your goal is to achieve a smooth and seamless slide from the top to the bottom of your range. Try to achieve a slight burning sensation in your stomach muscles before sliding. This should happen before you run out of breath. This is physical proof that you are strengthening the stomach muscles.

While performing this exercise, make the most out of every pitch. Regardless which note you are singing, at that particular moment, it is the only note that matters. Put everything you have into each and every note. Keep in mind that each exercise in this method is equally important. You may like one exercise better than another, but don't slack on any of them.

There are four important benefits from this exercise:
>   **1.** You are preparing your cords for full voice exercises.
>   **2.** You are improving your breath support and increasing your breath capacity.
>   **3.** You will be increasing your falsetto range through concentration and visualization, and...
>   **4.** You are smoothing out any break in your voice throughout your entire range. This exercise, therefore, is extremely important, especially to the development of your full voice. Now let's review:

>   1. Starting on your point of reference, sustain a light, clear falsetto tone on "*ah*" as in "*father*."

>   2. Concentrate on the **inhalation** and **yawning sensations**, while visualizing your **core of resonance**.

>   3. After the stomach muscles begin to burn, slide down to the bottom of your range, while visualizing your **core of resonance** sliding down as well.

That's it. Sounds like a lot, doesn't it? It's really not, once you become accustomed to the exercise. When starting the first week practice, you'll want to go up the scale as high as physically comfortable. It may only be 3-4 notes up the scale, or it could be more.

Regardless of your previous range, don't be discouraged. As you progress, the higher notes will come. When they do, you'll find that the lower notes, which were once hard to reach, have suddenly become much easier.

The key to increasing your falsetto range through this exercise is to make sure you sustain each note as soft and clear as possible with a minimal amount of breath pressure.

Falsetto is typically recognized by the breathy sound. I can't repeat this enough-Try to eliminate as much breathiness as possible and keep the tone clear during this exercise. When you reach the highest note of the exercise for the day, you have just completed one half of the exercise. The first half of this exercise is called *upscale*. You will now need to work your way back down the scale to your starting position. If you make it to an A4, repeat the whole exercise in reverse, beginning on A4, until you reach the note on which you started, also known as your point of reference. The second half is called *downscale*. When vocalizing downscale the following steps should be followed:

1. Starting on your highest vocalized note, sustain a falsetto tone lightly and evenly on "*ah*" as in "*father.*"

2. After the stomach muscles begin to burn, slowly slide down to the bottom of your range.

3. After a brief pause at the bottom, start sliding up the scale to your beginning pitch.

Don't forget your visualizations. When you slide back up, your **core of resonance** should also rise. Focus on the **inhalation** and **yawning sensations**. When performing the Falsetto Slide downscale, your vocal cords unzip and re-zip, assuring the proper development of muscular coordination in both directions. Now that your falsetto has been properly worked out and warmed up, you are ready for a more demanding exercise. **Falsetto Slide Example**

18 Transcending Tone

Transcending tone is a term I coined to describe the transition from falsetto into full voice. This is actually an old-Italian exercise called "Mesa Di Voce'." You'll start in a very soft falsetto tone then swell the sound of your voice until you reach a loud, resonant, full voice tone. Your goal is to transcend from a soft, light sound, into a full, resonant sound.

Transcending tone will be the most challenging exercise to perform. It takes incredible muscular control. Mastering this exercise is an accomplishment in itself. Your voice would improve from this one exercise, but the whole vocal routine in this book is critical for achieving your maximum voice potential. The purpose of this exercise is to develop the muscles involved in sustaining vocal cord tension. You will develop the ability to transcend your vocal cords from a loose vocal cord tension (falsetto) into a tight tension (full voice).

Start on your point of reference (C4 for males, F4 for females) and sustain the "*a* " vowel sound, as in the word "*play.*" Begin this exercise in falsetto then swell the sound until it becomes as loud as comfortably possible. Your aim is to go from one volume extreme to the other, (without locking your stomach muscles) while increasing resonance from minimum to maximum. This is similar to turning the volume level control of a stereo system up from one to ten (Or eleven, if you're a member of **Spinal Tap**). However, do not swell the sound so loud that you strain your voice.

If you do strain, stop the exercise and make note of your limits. Start over again, making sure not to go past the point of strain. You must make sure that you are not swelling your falsetto. If you swell your falsetto, the sound will be loud and breathy. Increasing the volume of your falsetto leaves the vocal cords loose while increasing breath pressure. A loud falsetto only dries out your throat.
Loud Falsetto Example

Your goal is to transcend into your full voice by tightening the vocal cords and narrowing the glottis. **Do not incorrectly tighten your stomach muscles to transcend from falsetto to full voice!** Full voice should sound loud, resonant, and clean, with minimal breath support. You shouldn't notice any breathiness in the sound of your voice. Rely on the **inhalation sensation** while vocalizing, to keep from applying too much breath pressure.

Visualization enhances the performance, so focus, focus, focus! As you transcend from falsetto into full voice, the sound will swell and grow louder. As your voice gets louder, resonance should expand. Resonance makes it easier to sing any note in your range. To maximize resonance in your body, apply the **core of resonance expansion** visualization. This visualization coincides with the **core of resonance** visualization.

CORE OF RESONANCE EXPANSION

As you recall, the ping-pong ball is your **core of resonance**. When vocalizing in falsetto, imagine your **core of resonance** glowing about as bright as a dimly lit bulb, and approximately the size of a ping-pong ball. The light represents resonance in your body. As the sound swells, your **core of resonance** should become brighter, much like turning up a dimmer switch. When the sound is loud and in full voice, your **core of resonance** should be as bright as the sun, radiating throughout your entire body. At the same time, imagine your **core of resonance** growing from the size of a ping-pong ball to the size of softball as you transcend from falsetto into full voice.

As you swell from falsetto into full voice, the ping-pong ball will grow to the size of a softball while increasing in brightness from dimly lit to as bright as the sun.

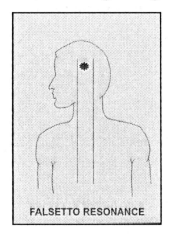

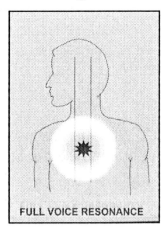

Falsetto resonance in head voice   *Full voice resonance in chest voice*

***Resonance expansion** basically refers to your **core of resonance** increasing in size and brightness.*

WHERE'S MY RESONANCE?

Resonance is not confined to the three main resonant cavities of the body. As the sound of your voice grows louder, resonance expands outwards, vibrating your entire being. When singing low notes, or singing in chest voice, your **core of resonance** should be low in your chest. To achieve the fullest possible tone, incorporate **resonance expansion**, while keeping the ribs expanded. This blends resonance from your entire body with your voice, with the majority of resonance coming from your chest. This works throughout your entire range. Wherever your **core of resonance** is located, is the most resonant point in your body, blending all other parts of your body with the core.

As the pitch of your voice rises, the **core of resonance** rises from low in your chest, to high in your head, depending on the pitch. This adjusts the zipping of the cords. When you perform this exercise, the **core of resonance** doesn't move, but **resonance expansion** does occur. With each individual pitch exercise you perform, your **core of resonance** rises a little higher.

In order to make the voice as full as possible, visualize resonance expansion! This releases any muscular tension in the throat and minimizes the amount of air pressure required to sustain different pitches. Do not push to increase the volume of your voice. **A louder fuller sound is not achieved by increasing your breath support. It can only properly be achieved by resonance expansion.**

When first attempting this exercise, your voice will have a tendency to waiver and break before reaching full voice. This is normal. You are conditioning muscles that you aren't used to using. Let's review:

1. Starting upscale on your point of reference, sustain a falsetto tone on the sound "*a*" as in "*play.*"

2. Swell the sound until you are in full voice, utilizing **resonance expansion**.

3. Continue to sustain the note in full voice as long as possible.

Continue upscale until you reach your highest comfortable note for the day. If you continue to practice this exercise, your range will increase within weeks, possibly days. Aim for the burning sensation in your stomach as you are sustaining the tone. This will improve your breath support, increasing your sustain time for long vocal passages, as well as increasing the muscular coordination needed to sustain notes smoothly and evenly. Next, work your way downscale:

1. Starting downscale, repeating your highest note, sustain a falsetto tone on the sound "*a* " as in "*play.*"

2. Swell the sound until you reach full voice, utilizing **resonance expansion**.

3. Sustain the note in full voice until your stomach begins to burn.

4. Then begin decreasing the sound of your voice back into falsetto, reversing **resonance expansion**.

It is just as important to coordinate the muscles to release the muscular tension required to tighten the vocal cords. This creates a contraction/relaxation relationship between the muscles. Not only does this strengthen the vocal cords, but it also improves the dynamics of your voice. Think of dynamics as volume control. Coordinated vocal muscles give you the ability to increase or decrease the volume for expression. Dynamics add expression and emotion to your songs. With the completion of this exercise, you are ready for full voice production.

Transcending Tone Example

19 The Siren

The Siren is a full voice exercise. I call this exercise **The Siren** because it mimics the warning sirens used to alert danger. This exercise was inspired by my favorite singer, **Jim Gillette** of **Nitro**. He does these incredible sliding screams from his lowest notes, up to his highest notes, without breaking. When I first started teaching, before I decided to use it as a main exercise, I used the sliding scream to get students to work through their break area. You won't use falsetto for this one. The purpose of this exercise is to eliminate any breaks and create a seamless vocal range. You are teaching the vocal cords to properly zip together. When done correctly, your voice will not waiver or break in any part of your range.

Start this exercise one octave lower than your usual point of reference position. This would be C3 for males, and F3 for females. If you cannot sing this low of a pitch, start on the lowest comfortable note of your range. Begin this exercise by singing the word "a" as in "play." Sustain the pitch for a couple of seconds then begin sliding up the scale until you reach one octave higher than your beginning note. If you started an octave below Middle C, or C3, you would end up on Middle C, or C4. Sustain the top note until your back, sides, and stomach muscles begin to burn, or until you run out of breath.

As you have probably guessed, you are also using this exercise to improve your breath support, so you'll sustain the note as long as possible. Do not strain your voice when sustaining the top note. The hardest part of this exercise isn't sliding up the scale, but sustaining the top note smoothly for long periods of time. In the beginning, your voice will warble and crack. In time, the vocal muscles will become stronger; the sound will become smooth and seamless, no matter how long you sustain the note. By holding the top note, you are teaching your muscles to hold the vocal cord position for that particular note. Sustaining notes for long periods will develop the correct relationship between your vocal cord positioning and your breath support.

If your voice breaks while sliding up the scale, stop, repeat, and **SLOW DOWN!** An unsteady voice is part of the learning process, but the end result should be a smooth, seamless connected scale. Just before you reach the area where you crack, **slow down**. This is the secret to learning to smooth out your so-called "break point."

Useful Tip: Slow Down!
The slower you slide over the break area, the more muscular control you will have to prevent your voice from cracking. *You aren't running a race, so take your time. If you slow down and your voice still cracks, start again, even slower, until you smooth out your "break point."*

To maximize your results, apply the **core of resonance** visualization. Remember, your **core of resonance** is the size of softball when vocalizing in full voice. As you slide up the scale, imagine your **core of resonance** rising straight up the center of your body, perfectly balanced. When you reach the top note, allow your **core of resonance** to float without any restrictions.

Continue this exercise in half-step increments. You might only work your way up the scale 5 or 6 notes in the beginning stages of this exercise. If you go further, that's great. If it is less, that's fine as well. Within a few weeks of serious work, you WILL notice an increase in your vocal range.

This exercise is easiest when done at a loud volume. (I'm not stating that you should sing loud, only that this exercise is more effective at a loud volume. I also do not want you to use a lot of breath to achieve this loud tone.) In time you can decrease the volume. Remember, you don't have to tighten the stomach muscles or push any harder for a louder sound; rely on **resonance expansion**. As your range increases, you won't have to sing your top notes as loud as you once did.

Useful Tip: Loud or Breathy? / Candle Exercise-
*You should know by now that more breath pressure isn't the answer for producing a louder tone. In fact, all tones, regardless of volume, should ALWAYS be produced with minimal breath support. So, how can I tell if I'm using too much breath to achieve a loud tone? An easy way to check your breath release is by using a candle flame to monitor your breath flow. Practice your exercises, or singing a song right in front of a candle. Your goal is to NOT affect the candle flame with your breath. If the flame moves, focus on the **inhalation sensation** and a buzzing sensation in the mouth for more resonance. This is a powerful exercise for learning to control breath release!*

Let's say that you have been able to extend your range to a B4, right below Tenor C, but you have to sing really loud to keep the B note steady and sustained. A few weeks later, you are able to sing a Tenor high C, or C5, and you notice that you don't have to sing B4 as loud as you used to. What's amazing is that A#4 is even easier to sing. Even more amazing is the fact that singing an A4 is suddenly a breeze.

When you reach your highest pitch for this exercise, work your way back down the scale to your original position. This time, you must complete **The Siren**. You should start on the bottom note, slide an octave higher then slide down the scale to the original position. Let's review:

1. Starting one octave below your point of reference, sustain your lowest note, on "*a* " as in "*play.*"

2. Maintaining full voice, slide up one octave from your starting position, visualizing your **core of resonance** rising.

3. Sustain this pitch as long as possible, to achieve stomach muscle burn.

As always, apply the **core of resonance** visualization to this exercise while adding **resonance expansion**. Maintain the **inhalation sensation** to prevent from over-tightening the stomach muscles. This assures a full, resonant voice throughout your entire range. As always, maintain the **yawning sensation** to keep the tongue low. The tongue has a tendency to rise on higher notes, cutting off the vocal path. After you reach your highest note, work back downscale as follows:

1. Starting downscale, sustain a full voice tone one octave below your highest note on the sound "*a* " as in "*play.*"

2. Maintaining full voice, slide up the scale one octave from your starting position.

3. Sustain this pitch until the stomach muscles begin to burn.

4. At this point, slide down the scale to your starting position, completing **The Siren**. **<u>Siren Example</u>**

When performing the downscale part of this exercise, you are zipping and unzipping the vocal cords, gaining complete muscular control over your entire vocal range. Eventually you will reach a point where you can comfortably cover two octaves in one siren. Let's say that your lowest note is an F3 below Middle C. Start this exercise on your lowest note, which in this case is the F3. Over the course of several months you increase your vocal range from an A4 to an F5 in the Alto range. When you are doing **The Siren** and you reach your highest note, which is now F5 above Tenor C, you would not start an octave lower on F4, but two octaves lower on your lowest note, which is an F3.

This allows you to cover two octaves, working out your entire range in one **Siren**. When you can cover two octaves, you have performed an incredible feat. You are well on your way to mastering your voice. The higher you can sing, the easier you can sing throughout your entire range. You may reach notes in practice that might not apply to your style of singing, but your lower and mid- range will become stronger. When you reach three octaves, you will be ready for the vocal Olympics!

Useful Tip: Hold Those Notes!

Hold your notes as long as you can. (Don't forget reverse breathing.) You are developing breath control. You might think you are increasing lung capacity but you are actually teaching the body to sustain a note with less breath. Let's say that you are able to sustain a G4 above middle C for ten seconds. Eventually you can sustain that same note for twenty seconds. You are now producing the same pitch with about half the breath pressure that you once did. Not only can you hold the note twice as long but there is also a lot less stress on the vocal cords from breath pressure, which means that you are protecting your voice from harm.

Useful Tip: All Notes Are Created Equal-

Most singers reach for higher notes. The key is to let the voice float above the note as opposed to reaching up to the note. When you reach for a note, you'll most likely end up straining. If I catch a student reaching up for a note during practice, I'll make them sway their bodies from side to side as they perform an exercise. Let me explain-If you are performing an exercise, like the **Siren***, begin the exercise by leaning to the left on the low note, and sway your body towards your right (switch your weight to your right foot) as you ascend towards the high note. The idea is to realize that all notes should be presented horizontally, like keys on a piano, instead of vertical (low to high). I can press any note on a piano without straining my hand, just by moving to the left for the low notes and to the right for the high notes. In this way, you won't think that you have to reach up to hit the high note.*

Useful Tip: Four Weeks of Techniques/Seven Week Training Program-

Here is a seven-week program for developing a powerful voice by using the **Raise Your Voice** *method. This is the same approach that I use in teaching my students, with the first four weeks focused on progressively studying the techniques presented in this book.*

Let me start by saying that if you are truly serious about developing your voice to your fullest potential, I suggest that you adopt a five-day exercise routine consisting of a cardiovascular workout (yoga, treadmill, swimming, aerobics, etc...) for strengthening the lungs, and an abdominal workout (sit ups, crunches, etc...) for strengthening the stomach muscles.

RAISE YOUR VOICE

*A strong set of lungs and abs are essential for developing a powerful voice! Today, I walked on the treadmill for just 10 minutes, did 100 sit-ups, performed the **Vocal Stress Release** program, and then shattered glass #31. Now, if that doesn't get you motivated and convince you that this system works, I don't believe anything will!*

Here's how the seven week program works-

1. *Week One-Perform the **Vocal Stress Release** program for six days with one day of vocal rest. After you have completed your warm up routine, you might want to sing a few songs to work on developing your vocal stamina. Re-read **Part One** of this book.*

2. *Week Two-Perform the **Vocal Stress Release** program and add the **Falsetto Slide** exercise. Same routine-six days on, one day off. Re-read **Part Two** of this book.*

3. *Week Three- Perform **VSR** and add the **Transcending Tone** exercise. DO NOT perform the **Falsetto Slide** during this week, only concentrate on perfecting the **Transcending Tone** exercise. Six days on, and one day off. Re-read **Part Three** of this book.*

4. *Week Four-Perform the **VSR** program and add the **Siren** exercise. DO NOT perform either the **Falsetto Slide** or the **Transcending Tone** exercises. Concentrate on perfecting the **Siren**. Six days on, one day off.*

5. *Weeks Five & Six-These two weeks will be intense. Now you will perform the **VSR** program along with ALL THREE exercises, every day for two weeks straight. There will be no break days, unless absolutely necessary! That means you will do this routine for fourteen days straight. The only way I'll let you take time off is if you develop laryngitis. Remember kids, you CAN sing with a cold! Oh yeah, one more thing... RE-READ THE ENTIRE BOOK!*

6. *Week Seven- Congratulations, you have reached the week that will set the course for your vocal training schedule. From now on you will follow a three-day cycle, twice a week, which equals six days. Everyday, you will be required to perform the **Vocal Stress Release** program for your warm up. Each day alternate between the three main exercises, i.e., day one-**Falsetto Slide**, day two-**Transcending Tone**, day three-**Siren**, repeat for days four, five, six...*

Are you up to it??? I think you are. When you reach week seven, I expect you to adopt this routine as a way of life. If you want more, you can always perform all three exercises every day-this alternate 3-day routine just makes it a little easier to fit into your busy schedule. If you do perform all of the exercises per day, then I will allow you to take two days off per week. The choice is yours.

Useful Tip: Starting Downscale at the Bottom-

One final thought. If it is easier for you to perform the second half of each exercise (downscale) by starting at the bottom of the scale (point of reference) as opposed to working your way back down the scale, by all means, go right ahead. Either way will accomplish the same result. Good Luck!!!

Useful Tip: Checking for Tension Underneath the Chin-

The muscles right underneath the chin play an important role in range. The muscles will slightly tense as you ascend the scale but should not tighten or "lock up" when singing higher pitches. If this happens, you WILL end up straining your voice. To check for tight muscles, stick the tip of your thumb up underneath the chin as you sing a song or practice your exercises. If the muscles begin to tighten, massage the area with your thumb and focus on the thought of relaxing that area. Concentration will help to relieve the muscles tension.

Useful Tip: Don't Forget the Mirror-

If you find yourself straining when practicing, don't forget to utilize a mirror to check the face and body for unnecessary muscle strain. You might be clenching your face or leaning back when reaching for high notes. I'm not saying that all of these movements will cause stress, but if you develop a muscle memory like associating a high note with leaning back and raising your eyebrows, chances are, you WILL strain and you will then only be able to hit high notes when raising your eyebrows and leaning back. You don't want to develop a tension producing habit to sing. Watching yourself in the mirror is self-analysis and will help you to break bad habits before they affect your singing voice.

20 The Keys To The High Note Kingdom

I have saved this chapter until you had a firm grasp of the requirements of singing. By now, you should have a thorough understanding of the voice. You should know how to care for and protect your voice, and should be exercising daily. Throughout the book, I have mentioned several keys to achieving you maximum voice potential. If you use these keys, you will unlock the doorway to the voice you've always imagined. I would like to present a way to easily remember these keys so that you can apply them to your vocal routine, to singing, and to daily speech. If you can remember **The Three R's**, and apply the **Seven-Point System** then you are well on your way to vocal freedom and your voice will soar.

THE THREE R'S

The three R's are: **Relaxation**, **Resonation**, and **Reverse Breathing**.

Relaxation: Always keep your throat **relaxed**, regardless of pitch, volume or tone. If you tighten your throat, (like grunting,) you will close off the vocal pathway, preventing the sound from flowing freely. Think of the **yawning sensation** to maintain a neutral larynx position. A neutral larynx equals a relaxed throat. **Relaxation** allows the voice to work naturally.

Resonation: You want to produce as much **resonance** within the body as possible. Apply the **core of resonance** and **resonance expansion** visualizations to each and every note you sing. (Expanding the ribs helps.) **Resonation** (multiple echoes) is the key to zipping the vocal cords together. So, make your nose, ears, face, and teeth buzz.

Reversed Breathing: Always imagine that you are inhaling the note as opposed to blowing the note out. **Reverse breathing** is the key to true breath support. Always maintain the **inhalation sensation**, regardless of whether you are practicing or performing. It will save your voice.

THE SEVEN-POINT SYSTEM

Whereas, **The Three R's** are a quick reference to proper vocal technique, the **Seven- Point System** is a more thorough approach, referring to the seven secret steps to range increase and voice control. All the information in this book about taking control of your voice can be summed up into these steps. Follow these steps, in order, and you will free your voice:

1. Apply **maximum breath potential.** Take a deep belly breath, expanding the lungs from the bottom up. Keep the floating ribs expanded out to your sides.

2. Apply the **hissing sensation** to obtain proper stomach tension. This is the feeling of a sustained "sssss ", or can be viewed as blowing out a candle very quickly. *If your goal is power, (like in rock singing) I give you permission to tighten straight down with your stomach muscles (**Power Push**), like when sneezing.*

3. Focus on the **inhalation sensation**. Imagine that you are inhaling, instead of exhaling, while you sing. Keep the ribs expanded for as long as possible.

4. Try to maintain your center of balance by focusing on **correct posture**, for an open vocal path throughout the entire body.

5. Apply the **yawning sensation** to maintain a raised palate, an open throat and a U-shaped tongue.

6. Visualize your **core of resonance** within your body for correct pitch placement and proper **zipper technique**.

7. Visualize **resonance expansion** for maximum resonance production within the body. The more resonance you produce, the less stress on the vocal cords. Feel the **buzzing sensation**. When singing low, feel your chest buzz, through your mid-notes, feel your throat buzz, when singing high, feel your skull buzz, even if you get light headed. Above all else, **feel your face and teeth buzz**. If your teeth are buzzing, you are producing plenty of resonance. **The bigger the buzz-the fuller the tone!**

If you are going to live life as a singer, then live by these rules to achieve your vocal goals. Commit all these rules to heart!

21 Developing Vibrato

If you want to perfect your singing voice and enhance your vocal style, you must develop *vibrato*. Vibrato is a technique used to intentionally waiver the sound of a sustained note. Vibrato adds flavor and expression to your voice. Explanations of different types of vibrato follow:

PITCH VIBRATO

Pitch vibrato is the variation of pitch between two notes, usually by half step increments. Pitch vibrato can vary more than a half step and either up or down from the original pitch. Pitch vibrato is the only true vibrato and the #1 type of vibrato used. Pitch vibrato adds a rich, beautiful quality to your singing voice. It is to your benefit to take the time and at least learn this type of vibrato. The other three types of vibrato explained in this chapter are basically tonal and stylistic variations, for adding a certain stylistic quality to your singing. Pitch vibrato will make you a star.

The easiest way to learn pitch vibrato is by using a *metronome*. A metronome is a device that keeps time by producing several audible beats per minute. You can purchase a decent one for $40-$60 from your local music store. A metronome allows you to change tempo. Every setting of a metronome refers to so many beats per minute. A setting of 60 refers to one beat per second and a setting of 120 refers to two beats per second.

Starting with a setting of 60, sustain your beginning point of reference, (C for males, F for females) slide up and down, twice, between your point of reference and one half step below until you are completely out of breath. With each click of the metronome, you should produce two vibratos, which would consist of the four notes. Continue on up the scale until you reach your highest note for the day. Next, work your way down the scale, but this time change pitch directions. Slide up and down from your beginning pitch to the pitch one half step above. As you progress, work your way up to a metronome setting of 120. Once you have mastered vibrato up to this speed, you can vary the speed to match the song. Your ultimate goal is a smooth flowing sound wave of vibrato, nothing too slow or too fast.

Pitch vibrato example

Useful Tip: The Vibrato Hum-

A really great way to develop pitch vibrato is to add vibrato to your voice as you hum throughout the day. Once you have developed a steady vibrato by practicing the vibrato exercise, start adding vibrato to your voice when humming. This is such a simple thing to do and something most people do throughout the day without realizing. You can hum along to a song on the radio or just hold out a note as you begin to oscillate the pitch.

STOMACH VIBRATO

Stomach vibrato, (or "machine gun" vibrato, as I like to call it), is produced by tensing and releasing the stomach muscles. This produces a fast machine gun sounding vibrato effect, which was a very popular sound in 80's heavy metal music such as **Judas Priest** and **Iron Maiden**. To perform stomach vibrato, start by hissing out the air from your lungs as fast as you can. Notice how the stomach contracts inward. Without hissing, say the word "*hey*" five times in a row as fast as you can. Feel the stomach contract and relax. This is stomach vibrato.

Useful Tip: It's Like Starting A Car-

When working on stomach vibrato, it is helpful to think about starting a car in the winter, when the battery is almost dead. You can hear a "ruh-ruh-ruh" type sound until the car starts. The sound starts out slow, then "revs up", just like the car starting. Each "ruh" relates to one tension squeeze of the stomach.

When practicing this exercise, use a metronome, and work your way up and down the scale just like practicing pitch vibrato. Start with a metronome setting of 40. As you progress, you can speed up. Repeat the word "*hey*" four times in a row per each beat of the metronome, and perform four beats in a row. On the fourth beat, repeat the word "*hey*" only once. So basically, when performing four beats of this exercise you will be repeating the word "*hey*" thirteen times, sustaining the word "*hey*" on the fourth beat. After you are accustomed to performing this exercise, drop the "*H*" sound and only sustain the "*a*" sound as in "*play.*" Continuing to produce the "*H*" sound forces excess breath past the vocal cords, which is unnecessary.

Stomach Vibrato Example

JAW VIBRATO

Jaw vibrato is a slight variation of the typical vibrato sound. This is more of a tonal effect. This type of vibrato changes the vocal path by varying the flow of the voice through the mouth. Sustain the sound "*ah*" as in "*hot.*" To produce this type of vibrato, begin by chewing the sound, as if you were chewing a piece of gum. Over exaggerate the chewing by opening the mouth wide and closing the mouth almost shut. This gives the impression that you are saying "*yah.*"

Perform Jaw vibrato in the same manner as Stomach vibrato. Start with a metronome setting of 40, and increase the speed as you progress. With each beat represents repeat the word "*yah*" four times and perform four beats in a row. As you progress, drop the "*y*" and sing "*ah*" to rid the voice of the undesirable chewing tone. "*Yah*" was only used to establish a working relationship between the up and down movement of the jaws and tonal variations. **Jaw Vibrato Example**

LARYNX VIBRATO

Moving the larynx up and down while singing produces larynx vibrato. This tonal variation is quite noticeable in Native American chanting. Start by vocalizing the sound "*a*" as in "*play,*" and with a metronome count of 40, work your way up and back down the scale to your beginning point of reference. Perform this exercise just like jaw vibrato, with two vibratos per beat. One larynx vibrato consists of lowering the larynx, then allowing it to return to its original position. As you progress you can increase the speed of the metronome. **Larynx Vibrato Example**

The different types of vibrato mentioned in this chapter will add quality to your vocal style. To maximize your vibrato skills, master each type. You can vary the types of vibrato in a song, allowing you to vary pitch, tone, and dynamics.

Useful Tip: A Great Vibrato System-
Brett Manning, *creator of the* **Singing Success** *program, has a great 3 CD program called, "**Mastering Vibrato**" that will systematically walk you through the "vibrato mastering" process. In my opinion, **Brett** is one of the best vocal coaches out today. This is the only vibrato program that I personally endorse.*

22 The Vocal Warm-up

It is important to warm up your voice before a vocal performance. Warming up your voice is like stretching your legs before you run. You should stretch out and warm up your muscles before performing any exerting physical task. To perform your warm-up, start with the **Vocal Stress Release** program, followed by singing or humming some warm up songs. If you feel you still want a more demanding warm-up, then you can perform the voice strengthening exercises as well. If you do, then only perform the exercises upscale. You don't want to over-do your warm-up.

Likewise, it is just as important to warm down from a performance, like a runner slowing down to a jog, then to a slow paced walk, to prevent muscle cramping. The vocal muscles and vocal cords swell due to the increased blood flow while singing. This is normal in all aspects of muscular activity. **You must warm down after singing just as you must warm up before!** If you do not warm down after a performance or rehearsal, your muscles won't have sufficient time to contract back to normal size before speaking. This could lead to a longer amount of time before you notice any increase in your vocal range, as well as a sore throat.

When warming down, your goal is to relieve any physical stress from singing. Singing increases blood flow to the vocal area, causing the muscles and cords to expand. Warming down reduces the swelling.

A basic warm down routine isn't as demanding as a warm-up. **Vocal Stress Release** with a few **lip bubbles,** basic **resonance hums,** and a few **gargling tone** exercises, is sufficient. You can delete the **vocal cord stretch** exercise from your warm down. Perform all three warm up exercises at least 5-10 times each, or until you feel that your voice has relaxed and you are ready for normal speech. That's it! If you don't warm down after singing, your voice will pay the price. Make sure that you take care of your instrument.

Useful Tip: Why Warm Down?

Why? Because if you don't properly warm down, your cords will not return to their normal size as quickly as they should and might become irritated and swollen. This is most evident the next morning when you wake up with a sore throat, or worse, not being able to speak. It would be similar to swimming right after you ate a big meal. What happens? You get a cramp. Warm downs serve the same purpose- allowing the blood flow to return to normal before speaking (or in our analogy, swimming), so that you don't get a vocal cramp! ☺

If you do wake up with a sore throat, performing a *morning warm-up* routine will help to soothe the vocal cords and prepare you for talking. When you sleep, the larynx relaxes and drops down into your throat, releasing vocal tension and allowing the throat to heal from daily stress. This is why the sound is stuck in the lower throat when you talk first thing in the morning. After a night's sleep, the cords aren't ready to jump right into conversation. Your voice is groggy and throaty in the morning and needs time to wake up too. Speaking from the lower throat and before your voice is awake is unhealthy.

The first rule of the morning warm up is re-hydrate your voice. I recommend eight to ten ounces of water when you first wake. **Gargle on tone** at least 5-10 times. You aren't aiming for range so keep the pitches low. After you have met your water quota, stand up, stretch your arms high above your head and let out a big wide yawn. Finally, perform several **lip bubbles** and a few **resonance hums** until you feel that you are ready for speech. **Humming helps to focus that forward resonance feeling in the nose, face, and teeth, to bring the voice up and out of the throat.**

> *Warming up, warming down, and the morning warm-up all promote a healthy voice and act as preventive maintenance. YOUR VOICE IS YOUR INSTRUMENT! Treat it with care and respect and it will last you a lifetime.*

Useful Tip: Neck Wrap-

If you have a stiff neck and are having trouble warming up, try this following tip: Soak a hand towel in very warm water. Ring out the towel, and then wrap it completely around your neck. This will help to loosen stiff muscles. Don't make the towel so hot that it burns when you hold it. If the towel is too hot, you will cause the throat area to swell, which is not the goal. Keep the towel warm and re-soak the towel when it begins losing temperature. Do this procedure as many times as you feel necessary.

23 Progressing Further

Once you have become accustomed to your vocal routine and have noticed improvement in your voice, you will reach a point where you will feel as if you aren't progressing. This is typical. In the beginning, you will have noticeable gains in range. Eventually your improvement will plateau. Don't get discouraged and don't lose interest. At this point, you must approach the vocal exercises with a different view. In order to reach your maximum potential, you must incorporate the following procedures:

LOWERING YOUR POINT OF REFERENCE

Your point of reference is the beginning pitch of a vocal exercise. Throughout the book, I have used C4 for males, and an F4 for females. You might have taken it upon yourself to change your point of reference in order to better suit your own voice. This is fine. It is necessary to adjust your point of reference to the lowest pitch possible. Incorporate your entire range into each exercise to assure that you work out the entire length and every point along your vocal cords. The more vocal cord involvement per exercise, the stronger your voice will become.

When performing the **Falsetto Slide**, start the exercise on the lowest pitch at which you can maintain a falsetto tone. Your falsetto will not extend to the very bottom of your range. The lowest notes of your range are produced in full voice with a loose pull on the vocal cords. The vibrations of full voice vocal cords are strong, even when the tone is produced at a soft volume. The breathiness that is present during falsetto will not be as noticeable on your lowest pitches, which is good, because you want to eliminate as much breathiness as possible from your voice. Your goal for a falsetto should always be as clear as possible.

To find your lowest falsetto pitch, start by sustaining a pitch in falsetto on the sound "A" as in *"play,"* then walk down the scale in half step increments. Do not slide down the scale from pitch to pitch. Keep each note separate. When your voice breaks, and you cannot maintain the tone in falsetto, you have found your lowest note. This will be the last pitch on which your voice did not break. If you have been using a C4 as your point of reference, and you walk down the scale until your voice breaks on E3, eight steps below, your new point of reference will be an F3. Keep in mind that your new point of reference isn't permanent.

RAISE YOUR VOICE

Depending on the health of your voice on any given day, you might not be able to begin on that low of a note every day, although typically you should. Don't let fluctuations in pitch dissuade you; always strive to lower your point of reference. With time, you could lower this point many steps lower than you might have conceived possible.

When performing the **Transcending Tone** exercise, the same rules apply. Strive to reach the lowest falsetto note possible for your beginning point of reference. By mastering the transition at lower pitches you enhance your ability to transcend at higher pitches. You are working your muscles and vocal cords in new and unfamiliar positions, strengthening the overall flexibility and coordination of your voice.

When performing **The Siren** exercise, start on the lowest possible full voice pitch you can sustain. If your point of reference for this exercise was previously an F#3, six steps below Middle C (C4), try to extend your voice lower. Work your voice down in half step increments in the same manner as you did to find your lowest falsetto note, keeping the pitch in full voice. When you have reached the lowest pitch possible, you have established your new point of reference for this exercise. Let's assume that your new point is a C3, six steps lower. Your point of reference is now two octaves lower than Tenor C, or C5. As you perform **The Siren**, you will slide one octave above to the next C. Continue the exercise up the scale in half step increments, maintaining a one-octave slide for each pitch. When you work your voice twelve steps up the scale, you will reach Tenor C. At this point you will want to lower your voice back down two octaves to the lowest note of your range, then continue the exercise. You will now slide from this pitch all the way up to the Tenor C, thus incorporating two octaves.

The wider range you can cover in one **Siren**, the quicker you will develop a seamless voice from bottom to top. If you have worked to develop your voice and have reached a Soprano C (C6), then you must lower your beginning pitch to your lowest note once again, thus creating a three-octave slide. That's an amazing feat!!!

When performing **The Siren**, maintain octave slides, regardless of one, two, or three octaves. This means if you start on a D, then slide to a D, not a D sharp, or any other pitch. This exercise gives the voice pitch structure. You are teaching the mind and the vocal cords the relationship between like pitches in different octaves.

128

With the **Falsetto Slide** exercise, you slide all the way down to the bottom of your range, same pitch being irrelevant. You are teaching your voice to smoothly slide from falsetto into your lower full voice, to eliminate lower break points between falsetto and full voice.

Now that you have a new set of applications for your vocal workout, I will present you with an extension of the **core of resonance** visualization in order for you to extend your range as wide as possible:

EXTENDING YOUR LOWER RANGE

This book was mainly dedicated to increasing the upper range of your voice and creating a healthy vocal mechanism. I have been asked many times if there was a way to increase the lower range of your voice. This question intrigued me, and I had a sudden desire to see if I could expand my lower range as well. I tried many different techniques. Nothing seemed to work. It wasn't until I applied visualization to the problem that I was able to see any progress.

I kept thinking that a lower larynx position must create a lower pitch. I should know that this was way off track! Still, this helped slightly, but attaining pitch should not require a change in larynx position. I turned to resonance placement, focusing on my **core of resonance**. If higher pitches cause the **core of resonance** to rise up the throat towards the top of the head, what would happen if the focal point of the core dropped below the diaphragm? Eureka! I had found another key. When I lowered my **core of resonance**, I was able to lower my pitch. For these lower notes, my **core of resonance** floated from my diaphragm to below my navel. This is harder than extending your upper range. It will require concentration. You should be able to feel your lower body vibrating. It will feel as if the sound is being created in your lower stomach.

This visualization can be used to extend your upper range as well. As you work your way up the scale and reach your highest note, allow your **core of resonance** to extend up above the top of your head. Allow your highest notes to float above you. This technique has helped me reach notes that I had never dreamed possible.

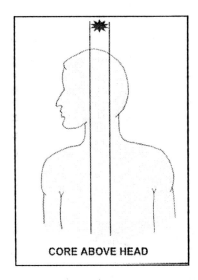

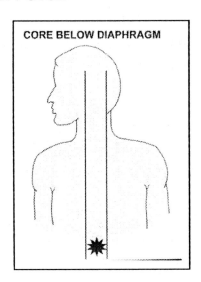

Useful Tip: Keep Those Ribs Expanded!

*When working on lowering my pitch and dropping my **core of resonance**, I find that it is easier to lower my pitch when I keep my floating ribs expanded out to my sides. This creates a larger chest cavity, which increases chest resonance.*

THE BULLFROG

One of the main questions I get from my students and through emails is, "how can I keep my larynx from rising in my throat on high notes?" Of course, one of the main keys is to maintain a yawning sensation." There is also a way to strengthen the muscles involved in larynx control. A great exercise for developing the muscular control of the anti-constrictors (yawning muscles) and deactivating the constrictor muscles (swallowing muscles) is the **Bullfrog**. The **Bullfrog** is a non-pitch exercise that strengthens the muscles involved in larynx control. Many beginning singers have trouble keeping the larynx from rising in the throat as they approach their higher range. An uncooperative larynx leads to vocal cord strain. If the larynx rises high in the throat, your vocal path will become narrow and constricted, which will change the tonality of your voice, and eliminate throat resonance. You don't want to physically control your larynx. You want to develop the vocal muscles to passively maintain larynx control, so your larynx doesn't control you.

Start this exercise by placing your fingertip on your larynx, then yawn. Notice how the larynx drops. Next, try to lower your larynx without yawning. When you can lower your larynx without yawning, concentrate on expanding the muscles under your chin, like a bullfrog expands the throat area.

130

 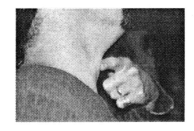 

HIGH LARYNX   ***LOWERING THE LARYNX***   ***LOW LARYNX***

Although this exercise is short and to the point, don't be fooled by it's simplicity. The **yawning sensation** might help to keep the larynx low, but the **Bullfrog** will strengthen the muscles that will enable you to "allow" the larynx to maintain a low position. If the larynx rises in the throat, you will "choke off" the vocal path. Let's review the exercise:

    1. Lower the larynx and expand the muscles underneath the chin, like when a bullfrog expands their throat.

    2. Relax the throat, allowing the larynx to return to its normal position.

    3. Repeat 50 times, in one-second intervals.

As you progress, increase the number of times you perform this exercise. I currently perform this exercise five hundred times in a row daily. As long as you have achieved muscle burn in the throat muscles, then you have worked out sufficiently. You don't have to incorporate this exercise into your vocal routine. You can practice this exercise whenever you want, as long as you perform it at least once a day. If you can maintain a low larynx position on high notes, your voice will flow and you won't strain.

*Low
Larynx*

&

*Expanded
Chin*

Useful Tip: Another Larynx Strengthening Exercise-

*Several useful tips ago, I told you how to suck on the inside of your lower lip to loosen phlegm on the vocal cords. This technique can also be used to strengthen the muscles that control the larynx position and vocal cord adduction. Repetitively suck on the inside of your lower lip for as long as you can, until the muscles in your throat begin to burn. Like the **Bullfrog**, don't overdo this one, because it REALLY works the vocal muscles!*

Useful Tip: Tongue Pushups-

An excellent exercise for learning to control an unruly tongue is tongue pushups. This "non-vocal" exercise will strengthen the tongue, allowing you to maintain a U-shape; thus preventing the tongue from rising on high notes. Begin by placing the tip of your tongue towards the back of the throat, on the hard palate (roof of your mouth). Apply steady pressure on the roof of the mouth (with the tip of the tongue) and slowly begin to slide the tip towards your front teeth. Allow the tongue to slide off the top front teeth. Repeat this process as many times as you can. The tongue will begin to burn in the center towards the back. This means that it's working! You are strengthening the tongue. After you have achieved the muscle burn, stick your tongue out of your mouth as far as possible and gently "clamp" the teeth on the tongue. Next, pull the tongue back into the mouth, while clamping with the teeth. This will "pull" out any knots or tension created in the tongue from this exercise.

THE SPEED ROUTINE

With each practice session, your voice becomes more adapted to your routine. Vocal cord positioning for each individual pitch becomes ingrained as a mental pattern. Performing these exercises is about muscle memory. Singing will eventually become a subconscious act as opposed to a conscious observation. Singing is like riding a bike; once you learn how, you never forget. (But, you still have to keep the voice in shape.)

The speed routine allows you to step out of your own way and let the subconscious mind take over. Some days your voice might seem like it doesn't want to cooperate. If things aren't clicking and you are losing focus, the speed routine will put the voice on autopilot. The speed routine is simply your vocal exercises performed at an accelerated rate. When performing the **Falsetto Slide** exercise, repeat each repetition as quickly as possible. Sustain your beginning pitch and immediately slide down the scale.

Do not think about what you are doing. This is a non-thinking exercise. Trust your voice. As soon as you complete one slide, move on to the next pitch, only occasionally stopping for a drink of water. When working downscale, as soon as you slide down to the bottom of your range, immediately slide back up the scale. Perform each pitch as quickly as possible.

The same technique applies to the **Transcending Tone** exercise. Transcend from falsetto into full voice as quickly as possible. Trust your voice to take care of the transition. If you have been practicing for some time, the exercise patterns will be ingrained in your mind. As soon as you transcend into full voice, proceed to the next pitch. When working your way back down the scale, return back into falsetto as quickly as you transcended from falsetto into full voice.

When performing **The Siren** exercise, begin by sustaining your bottom note and immediately sliding up the scale to your top note, and then immediately proceed to the next pitch. Use the same routine for working down the scale; beginning pitch, slide up, slide down, next pitch.
The speed routine exercises the mind/body coordination of the vocal cords. You can perform the speed routine at least once a week in place of your regular routine, if you so desire. It is beneficial on those days when you can't seem to control your voice and it is inconsistent. The end result of singing is to be able to control your voice without actually controlling your singing. Singing is a natural ability. Your voice should be allowed to flow.

PSYCHE YOURSELF OUT

As a final thought, I thought I would mention a few mental tricks I've used to gain those extra few notes when I couldn't seem to reach them.

Mind Trick#1- See the Zipper
Visualize the vocal cords zipping together from the back of the throat to the front as you ascend the scale. Take note that this is actually happening. If you continue to visualize in this manner you will eventually be able to feel and tell when this is happening. **A smaller the vibrating space equals a higher pitch.** You can feel the sides of the neck squeezing towards the center of the throat. This is a sign that the muscles in the throat are squeezing in towards the vocal cords.

Mind Trick #2-Mentally Change Pitches

When working your way upscale, pretend that whatever pitch you are vocalizing, is at least 2-5 steps lower. Let's say you've worked your voice up to an E above Tenor C and you are having difficulty reaching an F. Rest your voice for a minute. Then start again several steps down on C, but pretend that you are singing an A. Since your voice is used to singing up to an E, starting on a C should be easy. By mentally thinking you are starting on an A makes it easier. Your mind knows that an A is produced easily without strain. By the time you reach the F, you'll mentally be thinking D and won't strain trying to reach it. This technique works quite well for getting over those hurdles.

Mind Trick #3- Jumping For Joy

If you are in a vocal rut and you can't quite seem to sing a song or do an exercise without feeling any stress in your throat, then it's time to jump for joy. Just teasing. What I want you to do is begin jumping up and down at a constant rate while you are singing the song or performing the troubling exercise. This is just like jumping on a min-trampoline. In fact, you can use a mini trampoline if you'd like. Jumping will direct your mind away from vocalizing and focus on the jumping pattern.

Another benefit of this exercise is that every time you land from jumping your stomach muscles automatically drop down towards the floor from gravity. Jumping creates the same downwards pressure needed to perform a **Power Push**. So, get jumping!

TAKE A VOCAL VACATION

Even your voice needs a break from time to time. If you feel you have been in a vocal rut or are getting burned out, take a break. Take a week off and forget about singing. Don't forget how important it is for the body to rest. Every once in a while your voice needs an extended rest as well. If you feel you aren't improving, then maybe you have been thinking about it too much. Your mind could use a break from singing to clear out all of the clutter. When you return to your vocal activities you'll be surprised to see how well you sound and how great your voice feels.

The previous tips were provided to help you accomplish your workout and singing goals. Don't be lazy…Get busy!!! Ha-ha. Would you like more tips, tricks, and tactics for developing your best voice??? How about the secrets of rock stars??? Well, look to the right and start reading the next chapter!

24 Advanced Techniques

This new chapter presents the most advanced tricks, tips, and tactics that I have found for improving the rock vocalist's instrument. (This chapter is dedicated to all of you hard rockers and metal heads!) These are "secrets" that I have learned from teaching, interviewing rock stars, and continually researching for **The Voice Connection**. These are the secrets that singers who sing on the edge, use to maintain their incredible voices. I was originally going to use this as the basis of a new book, called **The Extreme Vocalist**, but I figured you would be too impatient waiting for the release, so I decided to give it to you for free, as an added bonus to this revised edition of **Raise Your Voice**. See, I could have waited and talked you into buying a whole new book, but I'm a nice guy, so here you go!!! ☺ Are you an extreme vocalist? Let's find out:

VOCAL SECRETS OF ROCK STARS

Since the release of **Raise Your Voice,** I have been asked several questions specifically geared towards hard rock singing. Everyone wants my "secrets" for holding notes, increasing volume, releasing powerful screams, adding rasp, and, of course, breaking glass. People ask, "How can I hold out notes like **James Labrie** from **Dream Theater**? How can I sing high like **Tobias Sammet** from **Edguy**? How can I sing with grit, like **Brent Smith** from **Shinedown**? How can I scream, like **Phil Tayler** from **Future Leaders Of The World**? How can I shatter glass like **Jim Gillette** from **Nitro** and, of course, **Jaime Vendera**?" So, here are the "secrets" I've learned through interviews with rock stars and world-renowned vocal coaches, and my own personal research and practice. These "secrets' belong to ALL vocalists, regardless of style. All singers will benefit from this chapter. May theses "secrets" release the extreme vocalist within you:

DEVELOPING A "CHESTIER" HEADTONE

How can I make my head voice or upper register sound fuller and bigger? The answer is simple-**add more chest resonance!** By focusing on adding a stronger buzz in the chest while hitting notes above an E4 for males and above an A#4 for females, you'll add more weight to the sound. The secret is to expand your **core of resonance** until it's bigger than a beach ball to incorporate all 3 main resonance chambers-head, throat and chest. Remember, your whole body is a tuning fork, so use the whole instrument!

You must also **keep your ribs expanded!** Typically, I always tell students to keep their ribs expanded throughout your range anyways. But, the truth is, the ribs naturally contract a bit as you ascend the scale, which is fine. Most students don't even realize that this is happening. But, if you desire that bigger sound, like an opera singer, as opposed to a pop singer, you must concentrate on keeping the ribs fully expanded. It's that simple.

DEVELOPING THE POWER PUSH

What if I told you that I could teach you how to increase your volume, enhance your vocal power, and prevent vocal cord blowout, with one simple technique? I bet you would have bought this book for that one technique. I call this technique the **Power Push**, and by learning and mastering this one simple secret, you'll learn to minimize breath flow, redirect the force of your voice, and increase your volume by decibels.

The **Power Push** is one of the best-kept 80's rock star "secrets" and is now heavily used by many styles. It is an EXTREMELY important technique for singers who want to sing high or with any sort of grit in their voice, regardless of pitch, which is why it is such an invaluable tool in rock singing and heavy metal.

So, how do I do the **Power Push**, Jaime? Well, allow me to first explain why tightening the stomach is so damaging to the vocal cords. Whenever you tighten the stomach, by pushing the stomach out, holding the stomach in, or locking the stomach, like grunting, you simultaneously pinch the vocal cords shut and tense the stomach muscles. This action forces the diaphragm upward, which forcefully expels air from the lungs. This forceful rush of air has nowhere to go except between your vocal cords, which are pinched almost completely shut. If this isn't a recipe for damage, then I don't know what is!

This is exactly why many singers who "belt out" songs frequently lose their voice. Singers have been mislead to believe that they must lock the stomach and tighten the throat whenever reaching for a high note, singing with grit, or trying to project the sound (raise the volume). Any time you tighten the throat and force air through the vocal cords, you are heading towards vocal disaster!

This is the reason that I was taught NEVER to tighten my stomach for high notes. But, when vocal coach and author of **"Strengthen Your Singing Voice"**, **Elizabeth Sabine**, showed me how to use this amazing technique, without locking my stomach and tightening my throat, I suddenly possessed the *power* to shatter a wine glass by voice alone. (It also takes correct technique, skill, (courtesy of **Jim Gillette**), and a lot of practice!)

RAISE YOUR VOICE

Now, I'm not the first to accomplish this amazing glass shattering feat; just the first **documented** *singer to accomplish the task. You could say that I am the first to prove that it can be done. I know for a fact that my vocal coach,* **Jim Gillette**, *accomplished this task way before me.* **Jim** *is a good friend of mine and doesn't care that I've set the world record. He's just proud that it was one of his students!*

The technique is very simple to learn. If you need more power, volume, or range, push and tighten straight down with your stomach muscles. This is the same feeling as going to the bathroom, or (for females), having a baby. Other examples would be the feeling that you get in your lower stomach muscles when you sneeze or cough. Think about it for a moment… The stomach pushes down and your butt cheeks (sphincter) pucker up.

Now pay close attention, because you must get this EXACTLY right for it to work. If you don't, you'll end up straining. The feeling should remain totally disconnected from the throat. **Don't lock your throat or hold your breath!** I know that sometimes when you are sitting on the throne, you'll grunt. When you do, you'll notice that you are holding your breath and you can feel the vocal cords pinching shut. This isn't the correct feeling. You only want to push down and tighten from the stomach down. Don't tighten ANYTHING above the stomach. Focus the tightness below the belly button and feel your sphincter tighten.

So, why does it work? Because, by pushing straight down, you are able to create a louder sound by tightening the stomach muscles without directly forcing pressure on the diaphragm muscle. (**Elizabeth** claims that our bodies are conductors of energy, and by pushing down we are creating electricity.) If there is no excess pressure on the diaphragm, there will be no excess pressure on the lungs. The only way I can think to explain the increase in power is to compare the stomach to an air compressor and your throat to the nozzle. It's like filling a car tire with air; you are providing a controlled consistent pressurized flow of air, through the end of a tiny nozzle.

After I mastered this technique, I discussed the matter with **Jim Gillette**. He said that he always tightened his stomach before hitting high notes. I wondered if I had been doing the same thing unconsciously all of these years. So, I put my hand on my stomach and started wailing. Turns out, I've been on the right track all along. I have always tightened my stomach when I sang high; I just didn't realize it. I believe that the only reason I was able to gain more power was because I became consciously aware of the technique and started paying attention.

Useful Tip: Feel The Power Push-

A trick to help you master this technique is to put your hand right below your navel and feel the muscles tighten underneath your hand as you sing. Maintain a constant pressure in this area when you sing. You should practice adjusting the pressure. The muscles should get tighter as you sing higher or when you sing throaty or raspy.

Useful Tip: Maintaining the Power Push and Expanded Ribs-

This one is tough. You'll need two belts. Put one belt around your chest (underneath your arms) and expand your chest and floating ribs outwards before tightening the belt. Once you have expanded the chest and ribs, tighten the belt just enough to keep the belt in place. If you relax the ribs and chest, the belt should become loose and fall down towards your stomach. Next, strap the second belt around your waist, below your navel. Tighten the belt while tightening your stomach downwards. Again, if you release this stomach tension, the belt should become loose. Your goal is to learn to keep the chest and ribs expanded, while maintaining a down-wards tension, below your belly button. It might help to put a folded washcloth in between the belt and your stomach to give you a point of focus for the down-wards tension. After using this process for several weeks of vocal exercises and singing, you should be able to remove the belts and maintain the expanded chest and ribs, and stomach pressure like it were second nature. Both techniques are EXTREMELY important to rock singers.

Useful Tip: Sing Out…Way Out!

When performing live, I find that as I perform the **Power Push***, it helps to increase the carrying power of my voice if I sing to a person at the very back on the room or hall where I am playing. This is the same technique I was taught when performing in "select choir" in college, because we were not using microphones and needed that degree of carrying power to be heard by everyone in the room. This will let your voice float up into the face and sinuses (the mask) and out through the mouth.*

THIS MOVES US ON TO OUR NEXT SUBJECT: SCREAMING!

SCREAMING FOR VENGEANCE- WITHOUT HURTING YOUR THROAT

Now that you have mastered the **Power Push**, let's tackle a common problem among hard rockers and metal heads…Screaming. If you want to scream your brains out without losing your voice, it's going to take some skill. If you want to learn how to sing classics like **Priest's, "Screaming For Vengeance"**, or **AC/DC's, "Back In Black"**, or if you want to tackle some of your newer favorites, like **Disturbed's, "Stricken**, or, **Saliva's, "Raise Up"**, it is going take some practice and effort.

138

There is an art to singing throaty and screaming, which could fill an entire book, but here are a few pointers and exercises to help you start the task:

The one thing that all of the professional singers that I have interviewed seem to agree upon is *vocal placement*. Vocal placement refers to the focal point of the creation of the vocal sound. All sound is produced in the throat by the vocal cords. But, there is a way to manipulate that sound, so that it feels as if it is being produced in a different spot. If you want to sing throaty, you must find a way to make it feel as if you have moved the sound away from the vocal cords, to prevent from squeezing the sound down in your throat. The change in focus away from the throat is called *redirection*

The best place to focus or "redirect" the voice when singing high or throaty is up into the soft palate. It's easier to place your voice in the soft palate when you focus on the **yawning sensation**. Some professional singers, like **Josey Scott,** of **Saliva,** feel that the sound is being produced below the vocal cords, right on top of the *diaphragm*. The diaphragm is the muscle along the edges of the lower ribs, right above the stomach. (You better know this by now!) Singers tend to tighten their stomach muscles, adding a little more vocal cord pressure, to get that gruff sound. I personally don't use this method, because I feel that you are adding unnecessary pressure on your vocal cords, but it seems to have worked well for **Josey**. If you decide to use this approach, moderation and correct breath technique will help to save your voice. Don't forget to use the **Power Push** if you choose (like **Josey**) to focus the tone down onto the diaphragm.

All the professional singers I have interviewed all agree on the fact that the throat must remain relaxed and open. If you tend to tighten or clench the throat, like grunting, to achieve a throaty sound, you are leading yourself down a path of vocal suicide. To maintain an open and relaxed throat, I want you to yawn. Notice how the back of your throat opens wide and the soft area of the roof of your mouth (soft palate) raises. This allows more room for the sound of your voice to escape and build resonance before leaving your mouth.

*Singers like **David Draiman** of **Disturbed** preach about the importance of an open throat. His sound is felt above his vocal cords as opposed to right on top of the diaphragm, with an open throat as opposed to a tight, clenched voice.*

ADDING GRIT AND GROWL

Now that you understand that you must keep an open throat, redirect the focus of your voice to the soft palate (or stomach) and apply the **Power Push**, let me explain to you how to produce a gritty tone:

When you produce grit in your voice, the cords thicken and slightly tighten up to "hold back" the breath. (There is also a slight narrowing directly above the vocal cords, to help produce that gritty harmonic sound.) This slight amount of pressure produces the gritty quality. This isn't the same as pinching the cords shut and locking the throat, unless, of course, that's how you've been achieving that sound (which is incorrect and dangerous). The cords are still mainly open as in singing clean. If you practice the **Raise Your Voice** techniques and the **Power Push**, you won't blow out your voice.

Here is an exercise for finding your grit and growl. I want you to sustain an "mmmmmm" sound on the lowest, softest tone you can produce (without whispering). This sound reminds me of waking up in the morning and yawning; the sound is very low and guttural. This is called a vocal fry. **Vocal Fry Example** When you create a vocal fry sound, you can actually feel the vocal cords opening and closing as they touch and release. Now, I want you to feel this sound in the roof of your mouth on your soft palate. The soft palate is where you must focus the feeling of all grittiness or growling.

Another way to get used to feeling the sound in your soft palate, is gargling. Try gargling some water, then try without water. When you can do this, switch between the gargling feeling and a vocal fry. I know that actually screaming a song, like **Linkin Park's, "Crawling"**, or **"Let Me Out"** by **Future Leaders Of The World**, will take a lot more energy and effort, but you must build from the basics. All vocal technique starts with a basic idea to build upon.

So remember, if you are going to sing throaty, sing with an open throat and direct the sound up into the soft palate (away from the vocal cords) while using the **Power Push**. If directing your voice down towards the diaphragm works for you, that's great! It's your choice. It's all about redirection: removing the heavy sound away from the vocal cords. Believe it or not, screaming isn't about tension, it's about relaxation and controlled direction.

Here is an exercise for learning how to add the right amount of grit to your singing voice: **Grit Exercise Example**. When first practicing this exercise, make sure that you only apply a small amount of grit until you are sure that you can handle the sensation. Practice adding varying amounts of throat tension, until you have mastered making this type of sound, WITHOUT pressuring the vocal cords. Focus the sound up into the soft palate. As the sound begins to swell and the grit becomes noticeable, start using the **Power Push**, and tightening harder as you approach a throatier sound.

*The **grit exercise** is a great exercise if you want to learn to add a little grit to your voice or want to sing throaty, whether singing **Aerosmith, AC/DC, Nickelback, Godsmack, Disturbed, Avenged Sevenfold,** or **Lamb of God**. This is the ONLY way to achieve a throaty sound without losing your voice!*

HITTING HIGH SCREAMS-CLEAN

Okay, but what about any tricks for hitting those scorching high notes? Well, if you've been practicing the **Raise Your Voice** system, you should all ready be there. But, one of the easiest, most effective exercises I have ever found for screaming my butt off, is the **E Scream Exercise** by vocal coach **Jim Gillette**:

The **E Scream Exercise** is a very simple and effective exercise. Begin by sustaining a low volume "*eee*" in falsetto, and slowly swell the sound until it is very loud and buzzing in your head. Start on any pitch that is comfortable for your range, and work your way up in pitch. So, when you do this exercise, it should swell in falsetto. **E Scream Example** As the sound swells and grows louder, you should tighten down with a **Power Push**. The louder you become, the tighter you should tighten your stomach. This exercise is better demonstrated by the master himself-on **Jim Gillette's Vocal Power CD**. If you wish to purchase the DVD, you can do so at **http://www.metalmethod.com**.

HITTING HIGH SCREAMS-THROATY

What about screaming like **Ralf Scheepers** from **Primal Fear**, **Rob Halford** from **Judas Priest** or **Brian Johnson** from **AC/DC**? The easiest way to learn this type of scream is to practice a variation of the **E Scream Exercise**. Instead of aiming for a pure clean tone, we'll sing an "A" vowel sound, as in the word "play", (starting in falsetto) and gradually add a throaty sound as we increase the volume. **Throaty Scream Exercise.**

Apply ALL correct vocal technique when screaming. This includes **resonance expansion (teeth and face buzzing), an open throat (yawning sensation,) reverse breathing, redirecting the sound, adding the power push, etc....** Start with a small amount of scream and hold on to the sensation until you feel comfortable.

As you become accustomed to the feeling, you can add more power and grit. This is how I learned to sing songs like **Back In Black (AC/DC), Hair of the Dog (Nazareth), Smooth Up in Ya (Bulletboys)** and **Broken City (Spread Eagle)**. When I am relaxed and my voice is warmed up, I can scream throaty all night with no problem at all.

Useful Tip: Five Important Points-

*Although I focus on ALL of the **Raise Your Voice** techniques, here are the five most important things for me to maintain my throaty screams:*

1. *Warm up with the **Vocal Stress Release** program.*
2. *Drink TONS of water! Screaming dries out the throat.*
3. *Maintain an open and relaxed throat by means of the **yawning sensation.***
4. *Redirect the sound towards the soft palate. This is like shooting a rocket and is easy when you use the **Power Push** to lift the tone.*
5. *Finally, Practice, practice, practice, all of the screaming exercises (clean and throaty). You will definitely reach your goal faster, while saving your voice.*

Useful Tip: Shooting The Rocket-

*A simple technique that I use to help students scream or sing higher is to tell them that the sound is like a rocket. When you push down, you ignite the rocket. If you are screaming or singing high, the rocket (**core of resonance**) shoots up into the head, effortlessly, when ignited by a **Power Push**.*

Useful Tip: This DVD is a Screamer!

*If you are a visual person and would like to see some screaming techniques performed, I suggest purchasing a DVD called **"The Zen of Screaming"** by vocal coach **Melissa Cross**. Melissa has worked with hard-hitting acts, such as, **Shadows Fall** and **Lamb of God**. Her method of teaching hard rock screams is very similar to mine.*

Useful Tip: Secrets of Screaming-

***Mark Baxter**, author of **Rock-N-Roll Singer's Survival Manual**, has released an mp3 called **"The 5 Secrets of Screaming"** that I highly recommend for all of you lead screamers!*

Useful Tip: Smile, Singing is Fun!

As funny as it sounds, smiling when hitting high notes helps to open the vocal path! This lifts the muscles in the face that tend to block and constrict the voice. Besides, you're singing for the fun of it, not for pain, so quit frowning!

ULTRA-SONIC HIGHS-Mastering The Whistle Voice

How would you like to add a whole new octave to your range-an octave you thought was impossible for you to reach? How would you like the "secrets" to accessing the whistle voice (the high octave range of **Mariah Carey**)? The extremely high pitches that she uses in her songs are easier to perform than you think.

When using the whistle voice, the cords are so tightly zipped that if you were to look directly at the glottis it would almost look like a pinhole. To achieve these notes, the cords must be "zipped" almost completely shut while you "blow" the air between them. The glottis is so small that the pitches are extremely high. When the cords are this tight, you only need the tiniest amount of air pressure to produce the whistle notes.

The easiest way that I have found to teach students how to hit whistle notes is to sing inwards. (This always makes me think of **Jack Black** and **Tenacious D.**) Try this-Start to inhale, then, as you are still inhaling, slightly clamp your throat shut. Did you feel the clamping sensation? Don't worry; this won't hurt your throat. **Clamping Example** Next, clamp the throat shut and practice "inhaling" pitch. **Inhaling Pitch Example**

Once you've become accustomed to creating high pitches while inhaling, let's turn the process around. It's time to practice creating a whistle note the normal way. Visualize zipping your cords almost completely shut from the back to the front, with a tiny pinhole opening at the very front of the vocal cords. Now, try creating a tone, while focusing the energy towards the front of your vocal cords-literally feel it at the front. It is tough at first, but it gets easier. The important thing to remember when attempting to create whistle notes is that you don't need to tighten the stomach or push for the sound, because you don't need power or much air for this register.

It also helps to visualize shooting the whistle tone through the top of the head. I have worked my way up to a C7 (and ten notes higher when inhaling the pitch) on the **Falsetto Slide**, so, I'd suggest practicing the whistle notes while using this exercise.

This brings us to our next exercise, which, I call the **Whistle Slide**. Begin by making a whistle note, on either an *"ah"* as in *"father"*, or an *"oh"* as in *"toe"*, and then slowly slide down the scale, while trying to maintain a smooth transition between registers. This is an awesome exercise for developing coordination between the whistle and head register.

Useful Tip: Focus the Tone-

*When practicing the **Whistle Slide**, try keeping a tight focused sound without any breathiness, like performing the **Falsetto Slide** exercise. You want to descend all the way down to your lowest notes in chest voice at a low volume. Visualize the tone floating down from above your head, all the way down to the stomach as you descend the scale. If you break between registers, start again and SLOW DOWN the slide!*

There is a definite difference between head voice and whistle voice. If you can hit a Soprano A (A5) in head voice, or as I like to call it, full voice, try to hit that same exact note with 1/10th the intensity and 10 times the focus. If the voice is shaped like a triangle and you are on the point of the triangle at that pitch, try placing the pitch on the tip of a pin needle; sharp, focused, super tiny, and half the volume as full voice.

Useful Tip: A Whistle Making Secret!

*An excellent exercise for learning to make whistle notes is the **<u>Guinea Pig Sound</u>**. By imitating this sound, you'll teach the vocal cords how to completely zip up to the whistle register. Practice makes perfect so practice imitating this sound throughout the day!*

LEARNING TO SUSTAIN LONGER PITCHES

I have been blessed with the ability to hold out notes for what seems like an eternity. (Well, when I'm not lazy and practicing.) Whenever I perform, I am always asked the same question: **"How do you hold out your notes that long?"** I always tell them the same few answers. **"Practice, practice, practice,"** and, **"If you follow the vocal training program from my book,** *Raise Your Voice,* **you will achieve the results you desire."**

But what if I told you that I have recently re-discovered a series of techniques guaranteed to improve your breathing. How would you like to be able to sustain notes for thirty seconds or longer? Do I have your attention?

Here is a simple exercise to strengthen the abdominal and intercostal muscles, while focusing on developing your **Maximum Breath Potential**. This exercise focuses on hissing. By hissing the air out, you'll strengthen the abdominal muscles.

Start by taking a deep breath in through the nose. Remember to breathe into your belly first. Make sure to fill the vase from the bottom up. Don't forget to expand the ribs by engaging the intercostal muscles.

Now begin to hiss, like a sustained **"sssss"**. Set your stopwatch and begin to hiss at a steady controlled rate. There will come a point when your stomach muscles begin to burn. It will feel uncomfortable and a little funny, like you aren't in control of your stomach. Don't give up. Just think; the longer you hold on, the closer you are coming to sustaining notes for long periods of time. You are developing stomach muscle control.

Now the tricky part is keeping the ribs expanded outward for as long as you can. Remember, this exercise is to help strengthen the intercostal muscles as well. If you can keep the ribs expanded while you release your air supply, you'll maintain a larger cavity in the chest, which in turn will slow the air release rate.

Next, try sustaining actual notes. Sustain the sound *"a"* as in *"play"* on any comfortable note, while timing yourself. This is basically the same principle you should be using when performing the **Raise Your Voice** exercises- holding the note as long as you can, until the stomach muscles burn. Don't forget to use the **inhalation sensation**, which is key to the development of breath control.

Useful Tip: Buy My Other Book ☺
*Want to learn even more about breath control and sustaining notes? Buy **The Ultimate Breathing Workout**, by me!*

HOW TO SHATTER GLASS WITH YOUR VOICE

I get tons of emails from individuals, who want to learn how to shatter glass, and have tried and failed. I want to tell you that shattering glass is NOT easy!!! That is why I am the first documented person ever to accomplish this feat. If it were that easy, I think it would have been filmed by now. Everyone asks how I developed this talent. So, here's my story in my own words:

On October 28th 2004, I received an email from **Jim Gillette**. For those of you who don't know **Jim**, he was the lead singer of **Nitro** and is unmatched by any other in range and power. (You should know that by now, this far into the book!) He has a 6-octave range and can sing louder than 120 decibels. **Jim** was contacted by **Linda Wolkovitch**, associate producer of **Discovery Channel's** hit show **MythBusters,** to appear on **Good Morning America,** on November 9$^{th.}$ The **MythBusters** wanted to prove or disprove the myth about a singer being able to shatter glass.

RAISE YOUR VOICE

Linda had heard that **Jim Gillette** was famous for shattering glasses with his voice by using an amplifier, and was hoping that **Jim** would be interested in flying to New York for the show. Unfortunately, (but, fortunately for me) he declined, due to his busy schedule. **Linda** was frantic to find anyone who could perform this feat. She asked **Jim** if he knew of anyone who could fill his shoes...

Jim is the only singer I have heard of, besides **Ella Fitzgerald**, who could perform this feat. Although I very seriously doubt I could fill his shoes, **Jim** told **Linda** that he knew of a singer and author who owned a website called **The Voice Connection**, that could perform this feat with no problem.

So, the email went something like; "How would you like to appear on national television, shattering a glass with your voice??? This is no joke and we don't have much time. Email me as soon as you get this message, if you are interested." So, of course I emailed him immediately, which was shortly followed by a phone call from **Jim**.

I was in total disbelief when he called. **Jim** had heard me sing years ago and had me hit a few high notes on the phone. He then said that I definitely had the voice for it and he could teach me over the phone. I talked with **Linda** that night and told her I would do it. The original plan was for me to fly to San Francisco on November 3rd to practice for two days, then fly home for the weekend, and finally fly to New York on November 7th. But, due to a change in scheduling with **Good Morning America**, the spot was moved up one day to November 8th, so I had to practice at home...

On Wednesday, November 3rd, I received about 100 wine glasses from the **MythBusters** and an amplification system from **Meyer Sound**. I sat up the equipment and gave it several tries, with no luck. Then **Jim** called me. He walked me through the process and explained the physics behind shattering glass, then told me to email him when I was successful. Within two minutes of hanging up the phone, I blew up my first glass. I tried it again to make sure it wasn't a fluke...By the time I had emailed **Jim** and he called me back, I shattered 6 glasses...

My practice and planning schedule was hectic. I shattered 19 glasses that Wednesday night, rested my voice on Thursday, and shattered a couple dozen glasses on Friday. I flew to New York on Saturday and met with the **MythBusters** that night for dinner. Actually, **Jamie** was already in bed, but I had dinner with **Linda**, **Adam Savage**, his wife **Julia**, and staff scientist from **Meyer Sound**, **Dr. Roger Schwenke**.

146

RAISE YOUR VOICE

The next day was non-stop work, but it was fun. We began by visiting the set of **Good Morning America**, then moved on to the **Discovery** building where I basically screamed at glasses all day long. Several professional opera singers from the **New York Opera** showed up to try out for the spot of my opponent on the show. Being a voice coach, I was eager to share my newly acquired techniques and was very successful in teaching many of the opera singers to shatter glasses by amplification.

By the end of the night, **Roger Schwenke** asked me if I was screaming as loud as I could. I told him no, because I was preserving my voice for the show. He then told me that I was well above 100 decibels and not one of the opera singers could get above 90 decibels. **Jamie Hyneman** was also concerned, afraid that all of the screaming was hurting my voice. I explained to him that by observing proper voice technique, I could sing, scream and shout all night, and would be fine the next morning, as long as I could warm up. If you have seen the video clip from the site, I must tell you that you haven't seen the whole video. The original video showed the opera singer we picked from the previous night's tryout. She was allowed to go first on the show, was given two chances and failed both times…

In her defense, I have to say that the reason we picked her, was because she had repetitive success in shattering glasses, (thanks to my incredible vocal coaching skills, ha-ha) and shattered several glasses the morning of **Good Morning America**, during practice, before the live appearance. It takes precision and power. Even I had trouble during practice because I didn't get a chance to warm up before exploding glasses at 5 AM. After her two chances, I walked on stage, screamed for about 10 seconds, and POW!!! It shattered!

That just goes to prove how incredibly important the **Vocal Stress Release** program is for warming up the vocal instrument! The **MythBusters** and the **Discovery** Network were ecstatic with my glass shattering performance. **Linda** told me that they wanted to do a full episode with me and believed that I could shatter the glasses without any amplification, and was hoping I would fly out sometime in early 2005.

Over the next few months after my **GMA** appearance, I continued to practice developing an un-amplified technique. I practiced the techniques from both of my books and continued to observe the way that the glasses would vibrate from the harmonic resonance of my voice. A friend of mine by the name of **Paul DeHart** would constantly urge me to scream at the glasses. He eventually started screaming at them with me and I dubbed him my "vocal sparring partner."

By the beginning of January 2005, I shattered my 1st glass and shattered fourteen more before flying to San Francisco to film the **MythBusters** episode. To prove that I could deliver the goods and inspire the **MythBusters** crew to fly me out as soon as possible, I decided to record myself shattering glass #8 and send the clip to **Linda Wolkovitch**, so that **Jamie Hyneman, Adam Savage,** and executive producer **Peter Engle**, could see for themselves that it was definitely possible. My diabolical plan worked and the following week, scheduling was planned for my trip.

When filming the episode, I shattered glass #16, officially making me the first person in history ever documented to shatter a glass by voice alone. As of this moment as I am typing on my laptop, I have shattered a total of 37 glasses by voice alone, and over 60 glasses with the aid of amplification, (including most recently, several shattered glass for the new **Sonic1** toothbrush infomercial.)

Useful Tip: The Dirt on Shattering Glass-

*The best way to learn how to shatter a wine glass is to have **Jim Gillette** personally teach you. Somehow, I think I'm the only one he was willing to teach! The next best thing to having **Jim** as your vocal coach, is to buy his video from **metalmethod.com**. If you are still serious about trying to accomplish this feat on your own, you will need the following: crystal wine glasses, straws, protective eyewear, (and of course, both of my books- **Raise Your Voice** and **The Ultimate Breathing Workout**.) You should NEVER attempt shattering glasses without first developing the power and range of your voice or you'll risk the chance of damaging your instrument. The safety glasses are to protect your eyes from glass shards. The straws will help you to zero in on the frequency it takes to shatter the glass.*

Useful Tip: A Word About Wine Glasses-

*The glasses I use are called **Schott Zwiesel** and are imported from Germany. These are the same type of glasses that **Nitro** used on tour and for the making of the "Freight Train" video. These aren't typical lead crystal wine glasses. They are titanium crystal wine and are considerably harder than lead crystal glasses. In other words, good luck breaking them. It would be easier to break a regular lead crystal glass as opposed to these babies. So, when purchasing glasses for practice, find a lead crystal glass that has a nice ring to it. If the glass rings when you tap it, it will be easier to break.*

Shattering crystal wine glasses requires the perfect combination of the exact frequency and the right amount of amplitude. The glasses I have shattered have fell between a Tenor high C and an Alto F, which is five steps higher. Every glass is different due to the individual makeup and density of the glass. Most glasses are not tuned to true pitch. For instance, a glass which might sound like a Tenor C# or 550 hertz might be slightly higher (550.3 hertz) or lower (549.9 hertz).

If you cannot match the frequency exactly, it will not break. It's like tuning in a radio station. If I wanted to listen to my favorite radio station, **WAMX, http://www.x1063.com**, I'd have to tune in to 106.3. If I tuned in to 106.2 or 106.4, I wouldn't hear anything but static. Get the picture?

Of course, the other main factor is amplitude. The sound has to be extremely loud. The glass I shattered for the **MythBusters** show took 105 decibels to break. The average trained singer cannot get above 80-90 decibels. So, don't be disappointed if you aren't able to shatter a glass by voice alone. There is still a chance that you can break one with the aid of an amplifier. We had great success in New York with singers from the New York Opera. I had what I consider to be the best training success with **Adam Savage**, when I coached him through breaking three glasses in a row, with the aid of an amplifier. So if you still want to try it, here are some pointers.

When you purchase your first crystal wine glass, try finding one that isn't very high in pitch, and has a resonating ring when you tap it. The more a glass rings from the flick of your finger, the easier it will be to shatter. If the ring of a glass dies quickly or sounds thuddy, it will be harder to break. It will still break, but you will have to work for it. The trick to shattering a glass is to increase this ringing or resonation until it overpowers the glass.

When first learning how to shatter a glass, you should begin by vocally matching the same pitch of the glass with a very soft head tone, or a light falsetto. It doesn't matter what vowel you use. I've used "A" and "AH", but prefer to use either "E" or "OO". Keep your mouth about three to four inches away from the glass. All you should aim for now, is to make the glass resonate by the sound of your voice. You'll need to learn how to sustain a long steady sustained pitch. This is why it is important to develop your technique. So practice sustaining pitches. Once you can match and sustain a pitch that resonates the glass, you need to increase the volume…A LOT!!! Make sure that you are wearing safety glasses!!! A much safer bet would be to set the glass in front of an amplifier. In fact, in all honesty, I prefer for you to use an amplifier for safety purposes.

Just because you can make the glass sing, doesn't necessarily mean that you have mastered the technique. At this point, you need to add a straw to the glass. As you approach the exact frequency, the straw will begin to dance. I have actually had the straw fly straight up out of the glass from the force.

If you are one of my determined students who still choose to practice without an amplifier, you can practice sitting the wine glass on a table, and scream at the glass from about 2-4 inches away. Practice making the glass freely vibrate on the table. If the volume is extremely loud and powerful, the glass will begin to vibrate and move across the table.

If you are extremely loud (like me, by using the **Power Push**) the glass will begin to dance and roll around on its' edge. When the glass begins to dance or the straw begins to move wildly, you are close to the exact frequency. Try to hold on to the note and add more volume, and, if you are lucky, the glass will explode.

Useful Tip: Woodshop-

Cut a board the size of the amplifier that you intend to use to shatter the glass. Find the center of the speaker cone and mark the center on the board. Cut a two-inch hole in same spot as the center of the speaker cone. Next, set the board in front of the speaker and line up the wine glass. Run a microphone through the speaker and start screaming! This will help to focus the harmonics into the glass, enabling you to shatter the glass easier.

That's as far as I can take you, the rest is up to you. The only way to achieve results is to practice. You never truly know when to expect the glass to shatter. It still scares me every time I break one. Just watch my face on the **Sonic1** infomercial. I know when I'm close to the thresh-hold because of the loud resonant sound of the glass. It sounds like two singers, singing in unison. When the glass starts to resonate and the straw starts to dance, maintain that exact frequency.

Be forewarned, that if you attempt this feat, I am in no way responsible for any damage that might occur. Although I have never been cut, it is still extremely dangerous. **Jim Gillette** personally warned me of the dangers of getting glass shards in my throat from the explosion. So take precautions.

Make sure you wear your safety goggles! You might consider putting up a mesh screen between you and the glass. I always wear safety glasses because you never know which way the glass will explode. Usually, from the force of my voice, the glass explodes away from my face, but, when I shattered glass #30, I got a little piece of glass in my mouth. It's definitely risqué and scary. If you wake up with a sore throat and a hoarse voice, don't blame me. It takes a lot of pressure to get the glass to vibrate, but if you are using proper technique, a sore throat shouldn't be a problem. If it hurts after practicing or the next morning, then your technique is wrong. It should never hurt. I screamed for hours both in New York and San Francisco before filming the amplified and un-amplified version, with no problem whatsoever. That comes from lots of practice and proper technique.

Now the rest is up to you. Please email me at **info@thevoiceconnection.com**, or leave a message on **The Voice Connection** message board to let me know of your results. GOOD LUCK!!

TOURING SINGER'S CHECK LIST

The following is nothing new to you at this point. The only reason that I decided to add this section is because I wanted to make available to you, the same exact checklist that I give to all professional singers when I interview or personally train them. This is THE list of essential voice pointers that I have given to more than 25 professional rock singers including **Brent Smith, Josey Scott, Tyler Connely, Myles Kennedy, James Labrie,** and **Brad Arnold**. It is a quick handy reference that you should print out and keep handy when are performing. It's your "vocal cheat sheet."

I-VOCAL HEALTH

1. **Sleep**- Sleep is very important. Try to get at least 8-10 hours of sleep if possible. Your voice needs time to repair from the night before. If your body is tired, your voice will be tired.

2. **Water**- Water should be the #1 priority for singers. Drink at least ½ ounce per pound of body weight per day. If you weigh 150 pounds, you need at least 75 ounces of water every day. Since you are singing every night, I'd suggest a gallon of water a day, with drinking water on stage. Singing dries out the vocal cords. The vocal cords must stay lubricated in order to vibrate properly.

3. **Fighting a cold**-If you are developing a cold, I suggest massive doses of Vitamin C and Calcium/Magnesium. Take one tablet of each, every hour until you start to feel some relief. Other sources-Golden Seal and Echinacea are natural antibiotics. These will help to fight infection. Colloidal Silver kills over 650 types of bacteria in the body and is extremely potent for fighting bacteria.

4. **Sinus trouble**- If you have a sinus infection or stuffy nose, you can flush the sinuses with salt water. Using a small ear syringe, (This is a rubber bulb with a needle nose end), mix a solution of warm salt water (only salty to taste, because if it is too salty it will burn your nose), then, suck the solution into the syringe. Tilt your head back and squeeze the salt water from the syringe into one nostril, until it flows freely from the other nostril. Repeat several times for each nostril until sinus congestion is relieved.

5. **Sore throat**-If your throat is sore, dry, or scratchy, there are several things you can use. Try **Throat Coat Tea**, by **Traditional Medicinals**. It contains slippery elm root, which is very soothing to the throat, and licorice root, which is natural cortisone and will reduce the swelling of the vocal cords. Zinc lozenges help reduce the swelling of inflamed vocal cords, as well as relieve sore throat pain. Zinc is very beneficial to the immune system.

Another aid is to mix one tablespoon of apple cider vinegar with one tablespoon of honey in warm water for a sore throat relief tea. Apple cider vinegar will kill the bacteria that cause a sore throat, and honey will coat and soothe the pharynx. If you need a gargle solution to help get you through the performance, mix ¼ teaspoon of salt, ¼ teaspoon of lemon juice, a pinch of cayenne pepper, a tablespoon of apple cider vinegar, and a teaspoon of honey. I'm sure you've heard that the citric acid in lemon juice isn't good for the throat, but a small amount helps to produce saliva, which keeps the mouth moist, so don't worry about it. Mix this in one cup of hot water and gargle several times. This solution will flush away mucus, produce saliva, kill bacteria, and coat the throat.

6. **Mist Inhaling**-When you gargle a solution, you do not coat the vocal cords, you only coat the mouth and pharynx. If you are feeling really dry, you can breathe mist directly onto the vocal cords. Purchase a one-ounce misting bottle and fill it full of distilled water. Open your mouth, then spray while inhaling deeply. The cords are in the trachea, or windpipe, which leads to the lungs. You will inhale the water directly onto the vocal cords. If you want something besides water, you should try Entertainer's Secret Throat Relief Spray. This spray contains ingredients that are similar to the actual secreted lubricants of the throat. The web address is-
http://www.entertainers-secret.com

7. **Enemies of the voice**- Just so you know, smoking and drinking alcohol harm the voice. Smoke of any kind dries out the tiny hairs that line the sinuses and throat, called cilia. The cilia act as tiny filters to prevent pollutants from entering the lungs. If you smoke, I suggest upping your Vitamin C intake, because nicotine flushes vitamin C from the body, making you more susceptible to colds.

8. Alcohol will evaporate the lubricants of the throat. Try pouring a small amount of rubbing alcohol onto your arm and notice how quickly it evaporates. Drinking alcoholic beverages do the exact same thing to your throat. I do know singers who will have a drink before they perform to loosen up. The problem is drinking too much, which will dehydrate the body, and relax you to the point of a drunken stupor and the inability to judge your vocal performance. If you must drink alcohol, drink wisely and make sure you drink plenty of water.

9. Caffeine products are also harmful to a singer. Caffeine is a diuretic, which causes you to lose water, this dehydrating the cords. It also creates thick yellow mucus that coats the cords. The cure- DRINK MORE WATER!

10. Cocaine is vocal suicide. Mucus from the sinus cavities will drain into the back of the throat and both numb and aggravate the vocal cords, causing them to swell. The problem is, you won't be able to feel or tell if you are damaging your voice by over singing, until the next day when it is too late. If you want to have a long career… DON'T DO IT!!

11. If you continually wake up with a sore scratchy throat, check with a doctor to see if you are suffering from Acid Reflux. This is an occurrence of the stomach acid backing up into the trachea, which will aggravate and inflame the vocal cords. This can be brought on by spicy or acidic foods, carbonated beverages, poor posture, or not thoroughly chewing your food.

II-VOCAL TECHNIQUE

12. **Warming up**- Warming up before a performance can definitely save your voice on the road. Here is a basic warm up that will loosen the voice and vocal muscles:

13. **Neck Stretch**-Start by stretching the neck towards your left shoulder with your right hand. Repeat the process on the opposite side. Next stretch your neck straight back, then straight down towards your chest.

14. **Neck rolls**- Roll the neck from the left to right, making a complete circle. Do this 10 times. Repeat in the opposite direction.

15. **Neck Massage**- Using your hands, massage the back of the neck, sides, underneath the chin and into the collar bone, making sure to work out any soreness or knot

16. **Tongue Stretch**-Grab your tongue with a paper towel and stretch it out of the mouth. If it is tender in the back, you are holding tension in the tongue and throat that can hamper your vocal performance.

17. **Diaphragm Massage**-The diaphragm is a dome shaped muscle at the bottom of your ribs that is used in the breathing process. Take your hands and work along the bottom of your ribs, slowly pushing the skin down towards the stomach. This stretches and relaxes the diaphragm.

18. **Lip Bubbles**- Lip bubbles are the best warm up exercises. Lip bubbles create "vasodilation", which means, that the blood flow to the vocal cords is increased, preparing you for a performance much quicker than any other exercise. Starting on any note, getting your lips bubbling, and after a few seconds, slowly slide to the bottom of the scale. Repeat this 10-15X on different pitches.

19. **Gargling tone**- Gargling tone is an effective warm up and helps to lubricate the throat. Take a mouth full of water, tilt your head back, and gargle on any note that is comfortable in your range. After a few seconds, slide to the bottom of your range. Repeat 10-15 times.

20. **Resonance Buzz**- This is an easy one. Close your mouth, and starting on a low note, begin to hum until you can feel the teeth, face and sinuses buzz. Sustain the note as long as you comfortably can. Repeat 10-15X on different pitches.

21. **Warming Down**- Whenever you finish the night's performance, give yourself a few minutes to repeat the warm up as a warm down. If you do not warm down, you risk the chance of waking up with a sore throat, or swollen vocal cords. Warming down is similar to slowing down to a walk after running. This prevents vocal cord shock. **Following are some "secrets" to help your voice on tour.**

22. **Secret#1-How To Breathe**- Most vocal strain is caused by incorrect breath support. Either singers end up pushing too hard to reach the note, blow too much air between the cords, or incorrectly over tighten the stomach. The first secret teaches you how to sing with less air pressure, which will result in less strain and the ability to sustain notes for longer periods of time. First of all, as most of you probably all ready know, when you breathe you should allow the stomach to expand. Most singers "chest breathe" or let their chest expand. This limits your air supply. Start expanding the stomach first. Pretend you are a vase and fill it from the bottom-up with air. When you do this, allow your sides and back to expand as well as the stomach, then the chest, if needed.

23. **Secret#2-Keep the ribs expanded**- If you keep your floating ribs expanded out to the sides, you will prevent the stomach from forcing the diaphragm back up to it's natural position. This slows air release, and gives the chest more area for a bigger sound and more power. Always keep the ribs expanded while singing.

24. **Secret#3**-This secret has allowed me to hold out notes for over a minute. From now on, when you sing, I want you to pretend that you are inhaling as opposed to exhaling. This is called the *Inhalation Sensation.* It's that easy... From now on, whenever you sing, you must imagine that you are breathing in. This gives you control over your breath support, helping to eliminate vocal strain.

25. **Secret#4-How to tighten the stomach**- If you are going to sing high or throaty, you must learn how to tighten the stomach for more power without wasting your air supply. The ONLY way to do this is to tighten straight down, like when going to the bathroom. If you push the stomach out, suck the stomach in, or tighten like grunting, you are doing it wrong!!! This will cause you to lose your voice. ONLY tighten straight down!!! I call this the **Power Push**.

26. **Secret#5-Supplements to take before a performance**- The best supplements for relaxing, strengthening, protecting, and opening the voice during a performance are zinc, licorice, and warm water/honey tea. Take a 50-milligram zinc tablet, and one capsule of licorice before performing, and sip hot/warm water with honey. The zinc and licorice protect the throat and reduce selling, while honey coats the pharynx and the warm/hot water opens the sinuses and mucous membranes of the throat.

These secrets helped me to recover my voice after neck surgery, and shatter a wine glass by the power of my voice alone, making me the first documented singer in the world to perform this feat. If you have any voice related questions, or are having any voice related problems, feel free to email me at **venderaj@msn.com**.

25 Developing Vocal Endurance

Now that you have worked hard on your voice, you need to put it to use. All of your hard work was for a reason: Singing! Hopefully you have been singing this entire time, but if not, there's no better time than the present. If you have been doing a lot of singing, you might have noticed an increase in strength and range since you started exercising your voice. If you have been doing a lot of singing, you'll notice that you can reach higher pitches during your vocal routine as opposed to actual singing. This is due to the fact that you have only been vocalizing on open vowels during practice. When singing, you are incorporating vowels and consonants at a rapid rate, constantly adjusting the articulators for different words and phrases. Be assured that you can sing just as easily and just as high as you do during practice, but it will take time for the mind/vocal cord relationship to transfer from practice to actual use.

In order to help the process along, you need to develop *vocal stamina.* Vocal stamina is the ability to sing any pitch in your range, at any volume, throughout any song, without tiring. As I have said before, the quality of your voice is dependent upon your health during any particular day. Your voice will tire more easily during the onset of a cold. But overall, your range should stay relatively the same.

The easiest way to develop vocal stamina is to sing every day. In fact, from now on, you need to incorporate singing into your daily vocal workout. Record three to five songs that you would like to learn to sing onto a tape. This will be your daily workout tape. After you have finished your daily vocal workout, proceed to sing along with the entire tape, monitoring yourself for proper technique. Use these songs until you feel comfortable singing them and you know them perfectly. The more you sing, the stronger your voice will become and the more comfortable you will feel.

You should continue to use the same songs for at least two weeks, no longer than one month, or you will become bored with the repertoire and will cease to progress. Once you start a set of songs, do not change them until you have mastered them, unless of course you feel that you might have picked one or two songs for which you are not quite ready. If this is the case, wait until you feel that you are ready to approach more challenging songs. When you have finished your first set of songs, move on to five new songs. Aim to challenge yourself with more demanding songs. In a year, you will have developed quite a song repertoire.

This is also a great way to improve your style. Usually, you would pick up to five different songs from five different artists. When working on developing style, choose three to five songs from the same artist. Pick an artist that influences you. Learning several songs from the same artist will help you to discover how an individual singer approaches singing. Take what you learn from that singer and incorporate the knowledge into your own voice. Do not try to emulate the tone and individuality of the singer. An individual's voice is as different as a thumbprint. Your voice isn't physically the same as that person, and you could end up damaging your own voice. Incorporate what you like about their style. Don't mimic their sound. You are not a parrot.

RECORD YOURSELF RECORD YOURSELF RECORD YOURSELF!

I really don't want to say it again, but **record yourself**! When you feel you have mastered some of the songs from your daily routine and you feel that you are ready to move on, record yourself singing along with each song so you can critique your own voice. Be your own vocal coach and be honest. Don't sugar coat the truth, but on the other hand, pride yourself on your accomplishments. You might ask, "What should I be judging?" There are several things to look for. Are you singing on pitch? Are you saying the words correctly? How about your breath control, are you taking a breath in the exact same spot as the artist? What about adding vibrato or nailing certain vocal licks? An easier way to make sure you are accomplishing these things from the beginning is by *song mapping*.

SONG MAPPING

Song mapping is a simple way to "map out" any song to create a visual picture of how the song should be sung. The following example is an excerpt from a song called "SKY" by the band **RA**. The lead singer of the band, **Sahaj Ticotin**, and his co-writer **Nandi Johannes,** have been kind enough to allow me to reprint these lyrics. I chose this band because they are one of the best bands on the music scene today. **Sahaj**, in my opinion, has one of the best rock voices I have ever heard. He has great technique, and knows how to use his voice. His voice is very resonant and strong, much like the voices of **Sting** and **Steve Perry**. I once heard him perform live when he had a cold and he still sounded amazing. When you can do that, then you know you've got it together. Now let's do some song mapping:

156

"SKY"

C#   G#- F#   F#   G#   E D# C#
Have   sure-ly   passed us   by ~~~~~

F#   F#   E   E
Poor   is   the   man ~~~

C#   C# - G# F#   F#   F# E C#   F#
That be--lieves   his   own   lie ~~~

C# C#   G# F#   F#   F#   G#
And the   sky   will   tell (me) ~~~ Sounds like "may"

Louder more Dynamic

C# C# E G#-F#   F# E
I'm not the on-ly one ~~~

C# C#   G# F#   F#   F#   G#
And the sky will tell (me) ~~~ "may"

C# C# C#--G# F#   F#   F# E
I   must be---lieve the sun ~~~

C# C#   G# F#   F#   F#   G#
And the sky will tell (me) ~~~ "may"

G#-F#   F#   G#   E C#
lo-ng   may you run ~~~

C# C#   G# F#   F#   F#   G#
And the sky will tell (me) ~~~ "may"

C# C# E--G#-F#   F#   F# G# F# E
I   must be--lieve the sun ~~~

As you can see, the first thing you should do is write out the lyrics to the song you are planning to perform. Leave several lines in between the lyrics so that you can take notes. Next, you should write the name of each pitch above each word. You can use a keyboard, a guitar, or even your pitch wheel to find the pitches. If a word has more than one pitch, separate the word with a dash. The word "**picture**" had several pitches, so I separated the word into "**pic---ture**". There were several words I separated, including, "**scripture**", "**window**", and "**believe**." The separation allows room for writing the pitches above the word and shows you where to change the pitch during the word.

The next thing I did was mark where **Sahaj** took a breath. I did this by adding a ' symbol. It is very important to mark and follow the breathing pattern. When you are singing a song, always breathe in the exact same spot that you put the breath marks. This assures consistency so that you won't run out of breath. Usually, you can hear a singer taking a breath, but some singers breathe quietly. This song was a little tough. I put breath marks where I heard them, and then added breath marks where I thought they should be. This doesn't necessarily mean that **Sahaj** was taking a breath at each spot, but this is where I will take a breath each and every time I sing this song.

Next, I listened to the song and added wavy lines above words that he sang with vibrato. The word "**picture**" in the first line had a quick wavy vibrato at the tail end of the word. So I added a **www** symbol to let me know when I need to apply vibrato. At the end of the sentence, "**I see in my mind**", the vibrato isn't as quick as on the word "**picture**". It is a little slower and more fluid, so I drew the symbol like this: ∿∿∿

If any words were sustained, I would draw a line to the right to remind me to sustain the word. The longer the line, the longer I would hold the pitch. As you can see, several of the lines had vibrato marks attached to them. I did this when he would sustain a word and then add vibrato at the end. If I didn't hear any vibrato I left the line straight.

I also check for dynamics. If the volume of a word increased, I would use this symbol: < If the volume decreased, I would use this symbol: > I didn't hear a lot of change in dynamics during an individual word, but dynamics did change during the song. I left a note to myself to let me know where the dynamics did change.

You'll notice that I have left several notes throughout the song. I give myself plenty of room in between the lyrics for this purpose. I try to keep the notes short, so I don't have to read a lot while I'm singing. In the beginning of the song I wrote "**guttural ah.**" What I meant was when **Sahaj** sang the word "**I**", it sounded like "ah." The word guttural means forceful and throaty. The word isn't smooth like a vowel sound; it's forceful like a consonant. He is applying style to the word and it sounds really cool. I put the first section of the song in parenthesis and wrote "**very breathy.**" This effect sets a mood for the beginning of the song. When he starts to sing "**I shut my eyes**", he switches to a strong resonant sound and increases the dynamics. It blows you away. If it weren't for the laid back breathiness of the beginning, the second section might not be as intense. This is an excellent example of an energetic emotional change during a song.

When you "map out" a song, jot down whatever notes make sense to you. I wrote the word "**pause**" in between the first and section sections of the song. This reminded me that there was a complete stop in the music between these sections. I also wrote "**louder, more dynamic**", to let me know that the second section had a lot more energy.

When I felt that I had completed my task, I listened to the song again as I read my lyric sheet to see if I missed anything. Always double-check yourself. Nobody's ears are perfect. I'm sure I have missed something or possibly misinterpreted something, but I'm confident with the product that I have created and I'm sure that it will help me to perform the song much better than if I would have skipped my homework.

You can check **RA** out at **http://www.raband.net**. For the purpose of this exercise, I suggest that you purchase **RA'S** debut C.D. "**FROM ONE.**" Listening to "**SKY**" while reading the previous lyrics will give you a better understanding of song mapping. Plus the entire CD is incredible. I guarantee that you will learn a lot about vocal technique by listening to this singer, and once you hear their first release, I'm sure you'll want to buy their second, **DUALITY**.

There you have it. Song mapping at it's finest. You'll be prepared for the correct pitch of each word, proper breathing, dynamics, vibrato, and sustain. Feel free to come up with your own symbols. The ones I've come up with aren't carved in stone. You'll have an easier time mastering a song when you write it out like a road map, so do your homework.

Useful Tip: Consonant Swapping-

*Here is a bonus tool for **Song Mapping** that I use with students who haven't quite mastered breath control and release. A very important lesson that all singers must learn is that singing requires very little breath. The typical scenario is that most singers release more air than is needed, especially when using plosive consonants like, "S" or "P." So, I created a formula for replacing "breath releasing" consonants with "breath controlling" consonants. Here is the basic equation:*

C&K=G
F=V
H=silent
P=B
Q=Gu
S=Z
T=D
TCH=CH
X=Eggs

*All you need to do when mapping a song is to use the above table and replace ALL "breath releasing" consonants, (like "F") with the appropriate "breath controlling" consonant, (like "V"). So, if I was singing the line, "**I painted a picture**" from "**SKY**", I would rewrite it like this: "**I bainded a bigchure**". I would rewrite the entire song and change any "breath releasing" consonant with the appropriate "breath controlling" substitute.*

*Take for instance the line, "**passing clouds of rain**". I would rewrite it, "**bazzing gloudz ov rain.**" Next, I would practice singing the entire song just like I wrote it. After I've become accustomed to the changes and have noticed a change in my breath release pattern, I would sing the song correctly, while maintaining a slight emphasis towards the letter substitutes. Because, after all, you don't want to sing the song with "breath controlling" substitutes, you only want to "think" the substitutes. If you think "D" and sing "T", it will still sound correct and you'll minimize breath flow and vocal strain.*

Useful Tip: MindMusic-

*The mind is a very powerful thing! A great way to conquer ANY song, is to listen along to the song and visualize yourself singing it, over and over and over again! Actually go through the movements WITHOUT vocalizing. Breathe in the correct spot, open your mouth and mimic the words, raise your soft palate, feel the **inhalation sensation**, push down for power, etc…Your mind doesn't know the difference and your vocal muscles will work like you are actually singing, while your vocal cords adjust to the correct positions.*

This last tip helps to develop muscle memory and set your voice up for a more hospitable vocal environment. Come on, trust me and give it a try!

Useful Tip: Swapping Vowels On High Notes-

Here's another quick tip for song mapping. Vowels can be just as challenging as consonants. Certain vowels, like E and O, are harder to sing in the upper range and can be "swapped" with what I call, "flowing vowels." These are vowels that open the throat and raise the soft palate. The E vowel typically lowers the soft palate, narrowing the vocal passage. Take the E vowel as in the word "feet." This vowel widens the mouth, because is produced with a smiling mouth position. This position narrows the mouth resonator and tends to splat against the teeth, causing vocal strain. You can substitute the A vowel as in "play". Yeah, feet will sound like fate, but no one will truly notice.

The O vowel is also tough. The rounded mouth position of the vowel "OO" as in the word, "rule", constricts the release path. If you substitute the "Oh" vowel sound as in "road", you open the tight-lipped position just enough to let the sound out, while simultaneously raising the soft palate. When the palate is raised, there is more room for resonance production.

The O vowel as in "gone" also causes problems. Although the soft palate is raised, it feels like it is pointed towards the roof of the mouth, like an A frame roof. The soft palate should be rounded, or dome shaped. Any constriction limits resonance and causes tightness in the throat. Try using Ah as in "father" to reestablish the dome shaped position.

The O vowel sound like in the word "foot", presents tightness problems as well. I tend to lean towards the vowel sound of a word like "fall", although not so much that "foot" sounds like "fought", but just enough to release any tension.

A vowel like "I" is considered a diphthong, or a two-part vowel. "I" is pronounced "Ah-EE". I usually drop the "EE", when singing in the upper register, and hang on to the "Ah" sound.

These are just a few simple examples. We're singing rock here people, so I'm not going to get into all of the correct usages of vowels as seen in classical music. This is just some of the tricks that I've found useful for pop and rock. For a more detailed description, check out other vocal books that focus on the correct pronunciation of vowels in the upper range.

26 Daily Vocal Routine

The best way to track your progress is to keep a vocal diary. Keeping track of your progress will help to keep you motivated and set your daily vocal habits to routine. By having to write down your vocal related chores daily you will be much more inclined to make sure that you don't slack off in the exercise department. I have found that by recording your progress, so that you can review from time to time, is an excellent way to build excitement and self-esteem.

On the next page is a filled in copy of the **Daily Practice Guide**. Here is how to fill it out:

1. Start on a Monday by filling out the date in the top left hand corner. Fill out each box in each column for every day of the week.

2. If you perform the **Vocal Stress Release** program, then check the box. If not, then put an **X** in the box.

3. Record your highest note for the **Falsetto Slide**. Then record your average-sustain time.

4. Record your highest note for the **Transcending Tone** exercise. Next, record your average sustain time.

5. Record your highest note for **The Siren**. Again, record your average-sustain time.

6. Record how many reps of the **Bullfrog** exercise you performed.

7. Record which type of vibrato you practiced for that particular day. Use **P** for pitch, **L** for larynx, **S** for stomach, and **J** for jaw vibrato. Also record the highest note and what metronome setting was used. If you practiced more than one type of vibrato, make sure to list them all.

8. If you are taking your daily dose, put a check mark. If you are taking anything extra, be sure to list it as well. If you forget to take your daily dose, put an **X** in the box. If you only forget a certain thing, put a small **x** and list the items, such as vitamin C...

9. Notes are very important. Always mention anything in particular that you feel has affected your voice. This could be a cold, or maybe just feeling a little down. On the other hand, also make note of any days your voice feels great. Every human being goes through a specific cycle. This is what is known as your biorhythm. Your body will go through a 28 period of ups and downs. Your goal is to figure out your individual cycle. Over a period of several months of keeping a daily diary, you will be able to track your biorhythm, and will know when your body is beginning it's down cycle. At this time of your cycle, you could increase your intake of certain vitamins and herbs to help maintain your energy level.

10. Finally, list the songs you are practicing that week. If you would like to make any notes about a particular song such as "I'm still having a little trouble with the break on song# 1", or, "Song#2 is really easy", write your notes beside that particular song.

DAILY PRACTICE GUIDE

	MONDAY	TUESDAY	WEDNESDAY	THURSDAY	FRIDAY	SATURDAY	SUNDAY
VOCAL STRESS RELEASE	✓	✓	✓	✓	✗	✗	✓
FALSETTO SLIDE	G5 15 sec.	G5 15 sec.	G5 20 sec.	D5 ✗	✗	✗	C5 Speed
TRANSCENDING TONE	B4 10 sec.	C5 10 sec.	C5 10 sec.	A4 ✗	✗	✗	D5 Speed
THE SIREN	B4 10 sec.	C5 10 sec.	C5 10 sec.	G4 ✗	✗	✗	D5 Speed
THE BULLFROG	100x	100x	100x	100x	✗	✗	150x
VIBRATO (TYPES)	P/60/64	P/60/64	P/60/64 L/60/64 J/60/64	✗	✗	✗	✗
DAILY DOSE (VITAMINS, MINERALS, AND HERBS)	✓	✓	✓	✓ Zinc Loz. GS Ech	✓ Same	✓ Same	✓ Same

NOTES: I finally did it! I hit tenor C on tuesday. I also increased my sustain time. I started feeling sick Thursday. My range went way down. I started taking Goldenseal and Echinacea and some Zinc Lozenges. By sunday I felt better, so I did a speed routine. I actually went higher with no problem. Also started doing the bullfrog 150x

SONGS: Sky / Ra - Good workout.
Separate Ways / Journey - Tough Song.
Like a sine / Audio Slave - Good song for Lows.
When will I see you again / Babyface - Easy song but really pretty

That's it. After you review the **Daily Practice Guide** print out your own copy from the back of the book, or just rip a sheet out. (I've included several copies.) So, print out your copy of the **Daily Practice Guide** now and start taking notes today. This is a map to your progress. You can track your range increase, your sustain times for breath control, your mastery of vibrato, and your vocal accomplishments through the songs you sing. When you look back over your progress, you will develop your sense of accomplishment.

What are you waiting for? I have given you just about every possible key I have found for improving your voice and you are still just sitting there? Okay, I'll give you a chance to review the glossary, but then I expect you to print out your **Daily Practice Guide**, grab your pitch wheel, drink some water, and get busy **RAISING YOUR VOICE!** Just remember, you'll only see a change in your voice if you actually apply yourself.

 Like **Jim Gillette** says:

"You wanna make it in the music business? Who doesn't? The only way you are going to develop the voice you want is to PRACTICE, PRACTICE, PRACTICE, PRACTICE, PRACTICE, PRACTICE, PRACTICE. I'M ONLY GOING TO SAY IT ONE MORE TIME! PRACTICE, PRACTICE, PRACTICE!!!!!!!!!!!!!!!!!!!!!!!!!!!!!!!!!!!!"

Make sure that you stop by my website, **www.thevoiceconnection.com** to let me know how you are progressing.

One Final Useful Tip: Follow Through!!!
*Your voice isn't going to change itself, so take **Jim's** advice and start to Practice, Practice, Practice! You cannot expect great things if you do not commit yourself to the art of improvement. Make me proud and bust your butt!!!*

Final Thought

I figured I'd better save this part until last so that you wouldn't get mad at me…After you've been practicing the exercises for at least 6 months and are feeling comfortable with the routine, I need you to take a big step with me…Forget about the visualizations. I know it's scary, but you can do it. All of this training was for your brain. It's time to rely on feeling. The **core of resonance** and **resonance expansion** visualizations were to train you to help reach your vocal goals.

Now, you must learn to sing from the heart and not the mind. Singing is a natural act; rely on the feeling of resonance as opposed to visualizing it. **Lajon Witherspoon**, lead singer of **Sevendust**, told me that singing, for him, was all about the passion! Singing can be a mind-game; so, don't think about it, just let your voice flow. You've worked hard on developing your voice and now it is time to sing!!! This doesn't mean to quit practicing the exercises. Keeping practicing every day, but rely on feeling!

Above all else, remember these words of wisdom from singer **Tony Harnell**: *"If it feels good, then you are most likely using correct vocal technique. If it hurts, and you are straining, then you are probably pushing and trying too hard."*

With all of that said, I hope you have enjoyed reading **Raise Your Voice**. Hopefully you have discovered things about yourself and your voice that has enabled you to expand upon your singing abilities.

Don't let your search end here. As I said in the beginning of this book, you can never learn enough about the voice and singing. I am continually searching for ways to improve my voice. I hope that you'll do the same.

If you have been working hard to **Raise Your Voice**, then you have earned a sense of accomplishment and deserve a pat on the back. But the real pleasure will come from the applause you receive from the people you touch with your voice. So, keep practicing, and live each day as a singer. The rewards will be overwhelming. Good Luck!

If you are interested in purchasing any products mentioned in this book, feel free to shop at **www.thevoiceconnection.com**. If you live in the Southern Ohio area, I am also available for private instruction, time permitting. Any questions concerning the techniques in this book are welcome. Just email me at **info@thevoiceconnection.com** Again, time permitting, I'll answer your email.

Glossary

Abdominal Area The cavity of the body between the chest and the pelvis.

Adduction The process of the vocal cords squeezing together from the back of the throat to the front, shortening the vibrating space.

Affirmation A repetitive positive statement.

Air Flow The release of air from the lungs through the throat and out the mouth.

Air Reserve The amount of air contained in the lungs used to sustain a lyrical passage during singing.

Alto A female vocal classification covering a range from A2-E6.

Analgesic A drug used to relieve pain.

Antihistamine A drug used for treating allergies and colds.

Antiseptic A substance that kills the germs that causes decay or infection.

Articulation The proper pronunciation of words.

Articulators The area of the human anatomy responsible for word production.

Baritone A male vocal classification covering a range from B1-A4.

Bass A male vocal classification covering a range from E1-E4.

Break Point The area of the voice between chest and throat/head resonance.

Breath Control The ability to control the release of breath between the vocal cords.

Breath Support The relationship between the diaphragm and stomach/back muscles that supports breath support.

Chest Breathing Breathing with the upper part of the chest, which only utilizes about 1/3 of maximum lung capacity.

Chest Cavity   The part of the body enclosed by the ribs and the sternum.

Chest Voice   The lower part of one's range that produces mostly chest resonance.

Chromatic Octave   A musical scale that covers twelve notes, in half step increments.

Cilia   Tiny hairs in the body, that act like small filters, to prevent foreign objects from entering the lungs, which line the sinuses and throat.

Citric Acid   A sour organic acid obtained from lemon juice, which is irritable to the vocal cords.

Core of Resonance   The central focal point of resonance, relative to pitch.

Decongestant   A drug that relieves congestion.

Diaphragm   The muscle that separates the abdominal and chest cavities.

Diaphragmatic Breathing   Breathing with the lower part of the chest, which utilizes about 2/3 of maximum lung capacity.

Downscale   A term for describing the second half of a vocal exercise, relating to working one's way back down a musical scale.

Dynamics   A term used to describe the increase or decrease of volume and energy of the voice during singing.

Elasticity   A term used to describe the flexibility or pliability of the vocal cords.

Enunciation   The proper articulation of words.

Esophagus   A muscular tube that leads from the cavity behind the mouth to the stomach.

Falsetto   A light breathy tone with little or no resonance, used in the higher register in place of full voice, which is produced by loose vocal cords.

Falsetto Slide   An exercise produced entirely in falsetto, which strengthens and smoothes out the entire falsetto range.

False Vocal Fold   Two protrusions above the vocal cords, which were once thought to produce falsetto.

Full Voice   A strong tone with lots of resonance, used throughout the entire vocal range, produced by your natural voice.

Gargling Tone   A warm up exercise produced by singing "ah" while gargling water.

Hard Palate   The bony anterior part of the palate, forming the roof of the mouth.

Harmonics   The musical overtones of the voice.

Head Cavity   The upper area of the skull, which produces head resonance.

Head Voice   The upper part of one's range that produces mostly head resonance.

Humidifier   A machine that releases cool moisture into the air.

Hydrated   A term used to describe when the voice and body have obtained an adequate amount of moisture.

Inhalation Sensation   The visualized sensation of breathing in while singing. Also referred to as reverse breathing.

Intonation   The rise and fall in pitch of the voice during speech and singing.

Jaw   The parts of the walls of the mouth, which open and close it.

Jaw Tension Release   A technique used to relieve stress in the jawbone area.

Jaw Vibrato   A type of vibrato produced by moving the jaw up and down.

Key   The tone or pitch of the voice.

Laryngitis   An infection and inflammation of the larynx.

Larynx   The upper part of the trachea containing the vocal cords.

Larynx Vibrato   A type of vibrato produced by moving the larynx up and down.

Lips   The two fleshy folds that surround the mouth.

Lip Bubbles   A warm up exercise produced by pursing the lips together and sustaining a tone.

Lungs   The pair of bag-like breathing organs in the chest.

Lung Capacity   The amount of air that can be held in the lungs.

Lyrical Phrasing   The production and articulation of a song.

Maximum Breath Potential   A form of breathing, which incorporates both chest and diaphragmatic breathing for full lung capacity.

Metronome   A device for marking exact time by a regular repeated tick.

Mid-range   A term used to describe the range right below, at, and above the break point, which produces mostly throat resonance.

Monotone   The act of repetitively speaking or singing on the same pitch.

Mucus   A slippery secretion of membranes, lining the throat and nasal cavities.

Muscular Tension   Muscular tension refers to either muscular stress or the small amount of tension required to stretch and zip the vocal cords.

Nasal Tone   The quality of sound when produced mainly thru the nose.

Notes   A musical pitch designated by a letter of the alphabet.

Octave   A musical interval covering twelve half step notes.

Oxygen   A colorless, odorless element found in the air that is essential to life.

Pharyngitis   An infection or inflammation of the pharynx.

Pharynx   The space in the back of the mouth into which the nostrils, esophagus, and trachea open.

Phlegm   Thick mucus secretions in abnormal quantity in the throat and sinuses.

Pitch   The highness or lowness of sound designated by a note.

Pitch Matching   The act of vocally matching pitches to improve intonation.

Pitch Vibrato   A type of vibrato produced by varying the pitch down and up by a half step increment.

Pitch Wheel   A small handheld instrument, much like a harmonica, that covers one chromatic octave.

Pneumonia   An infection or inflammation of the lungs.

Point of Reference   The point of reference refers to the beginning pitch of a vocal exercise.

Post Nasal Drip   Flow of mucous secretion from the sinus cavity to the pharynx.

Posture   The position or alignment of the body.

R.D.A.   Abbr. Recommended Daily Allowance.

Recurrent-Congestion   Reoccurring sinus congestion due to the body's tolerance buildup to nasal inhalers.

Resonance   An echo of sound waves within the body caused by the vocal cords.

Resonance Expansion   The enrichment and increasing of sound waves within the body.

Resonance Hum   A warm up exercise to increase resonance.

Resonance Placement   The positioning of resonance within the body.

Resonators The main resonating cavities of the body.

Reverberation The reflection or echo of sound.

Reverse Breathing See *inhalation sensation*

Sinusitis An infection or inflammation of the sinus cavity.

Siren An exercise produced entirely in full voice, which strengthens and smoothes out the entire full voice range.

Skull The skeleton of the head that protects the brain and supports the jaws.

Soft Palate The fold at the back of the hard palate that raises when yawning.

Soprano A female vocal classification covering a range from C3-F6.

Speed Routine A Vocal workout performed as quickly as possible with no breaks.

Stomach Muscles The muscles protecting the lower organs, used to support the exhalation process.

Stomach Vibrato A type of vibrato produced by tensing and relaxing the stomach muscles.

Straining The act of tensing and abusing the vocal muscles and vocal cords.

Tenor A male vocal classification covering a range from D2-E5.

Teeth A hard bony structure in the mouth used for chewing food and articulation.

Temporal Mandibular Joint The indenture in front of the ears, where the jaws open and close.

Tone A reference to the sound quality of a vocal pitch.

Tongue The fleshy muscles in the mouth used for tasting and articulation.

RAISE YOUR VOICE

Trachea The main tube by which air enters the lungs, also known as the windpipe.

Transcending Tone An exercise maintained on a certain pitch, which starts in full voice and develops into falsetto.

Upscale A term for describing the first half of a vocal exercise, relating to working one's way up a musical scale.

Vaporizer A machine that releases warm moisture into the air.

Vertebrae One of the segments of bone or cartilage making up the backbone.

Vocal Break A break or crack in one's upper vocal range. This occurs when the vocal cords have extended beyond their stretching point.

Vocal Cords Two elastic folds of mucous membrane, which are housed in the larynx, that vibrate together to produce pitch.

Vocal Cord Stretch A warm up exercise based on **The Siren** that zips and un-zips the vocal cords.

Vocal Classification A method of categorizing a singer's voice by the highest and lowest note of their range.

Vocal Nodules A small lump or swelling on the vocal cords due to abuse, that can only be removed by surgery.

Vocal Path The path of sound as it travels from the vocal cords, up the throat, pharynx, and thru the mouth.

Vocal Polyps A swollen tumorous membrane that might require removal by surgery.

Vocal Stamina The ability to sing continuously for long periods of time, without tiring.

Vocal Stress Release A specifically designed vocal warm-up program that releases stress and tension in the voice, and prepares the voice for singing.

Warble   A musical trill.

Whisper   To speak very low or under the breath.

Whistle Voice   The highest register, created at the very front of the vocal cords.

Yawning Sensation   The physical sensation of a low larynx, arched soft palate, and lowered U-shaped tongue that produces an open vocal path.

Zipper Technique   The visual and physical technique that helps to produce vocal cord adduction.

Acknowledgements

I would like to thank God for the inspiration and motivation that you have instilled upon me during the writing of this book and life in general. I have been divinely inspired, My wife, Diane-Thanks for standing by my side for the past fifteen years, and believing in my dreams, My son, Ryan-I am so glad that you've discovered music, My mother, Linda Fagan-Thank you for your help in cultivating my love of music, and allowing me to experience the music business at such an early age in my life, My uncle, Ron Hadsell Jr.-if it weren't for you, I would never have discovered **Journey**, or piano. I think they go together, my uncle, Don Hadsell-you've always treated me like a son. That's why I call you "Daddy Don." Thanks for not making me cut my hair.

To the best band that never was-Keith Gilbert, my best friend of the last sixteen years-You've always believed in me as a singer, Scott Stith-You've taken me to a higher path, Howard Turner-Where's your bass? Oh well, I guess we'll have to settle for harmonies, guitar and a piano, Matt "Sven Hungstrom" Hoover-Thanks for putting up with my singing all of those years. Do you remember when your dad said, "Jaime's got a voice that could hurt you"? I'm still not really sure whether that was good or bad.

Joyce Foster-Your guidance made the dream of this book a reality. We will all miss you, Charles Greene, my band director-I have never met a man with more love and devotion to music than you. You have taught me so much, Vicky Balsinger, my first choral director-It's been more than twenty years since I've seen or heard from you, but you will always be in my heart. You are the reason I developed such a love for harmony, Shirley Crothers, my first voice teacher-You helped me to begin this journey, Jim Gillette, my best vocal instructor-you have been my inspiration for writing this book. I'm proud to call you my friend. Thank you for the GMA hookup. I know that it's going to change my life. I owe you more than steak dinner, Tony Harnell- Thank you for your positive input, and your words of wisdom. You are a pure soul, Thomas Appell, Brett Manning, Roger Love, Elizabeth Sabine, and Melissa Cross-I am so glad that there are great vocal coaches to spread the love and joy of singing, Tony Couch-your belief in me has helped The Voice Connection to keep connecting, To all of the vocal instructors I have ever had, whether in person, books, videos, or personal conversations, I have learned from each and every one of you.

To my new friends from the MythBusters crew: Jamie Hyneman, Adam & Julia Savage, Linda Wolkovitch, and Amelia Zimmern-New York was a trip! Thanks for believing in me. I'm glad I was able to deliver the goods. Maybe next time I'll partake in a little "gerioke." Dr. Roger Schwenke from Meyer Sound; I told you to make me look good…and…you did! You're a friend for life! You are, by far, the coolest scientist I know!

Very special thanks to the people who helped me complete this project! Thanks to Sahaj Ticotin and Nandi Johannes, for giving me permission to use the lyrics for "Sky." Without "Sky", there would have been no Song Mapping, Molly Burnside for your dedication to The Voice Connection and helping me complete Raise Your Voice, Jason Burnside for the friendship, the artwork, and the video editing, Stephanie Keen-without you, I would never have finished this book! Your interest in this project made me believe in myself, Neil Tarvin; I know I've driven you nuts. The next book will be easier. Thanks for your help, Billy Guy-Thanks for teaching me how to use Cool Edit Pro, but more so, for being a true friend, Finally, to all of the singers who have ignited a spark inside my soul and all the singers yet to be born, thank you.

I would also like to personally thank each person who reads this book. It is my wish to enlighten as many people as I can with the knowledge that I have obtained over the past ten to fifteen years. I hope that you enjoyed this book and learned a great deal about yourself and your voice. God Bless.

Jaime Vendera

DAILY PRACTICE GUIDE

	MONDAY	TUESDAY	WEDNESDAY	THURSDAY	FRIDAY	SATURDAY	SUNDAY
VOCAL STRESS RELEASE							
FALSETTO SLIDE							
TRANSCENDING TONE							
THE SIREN							
THE BULLFROG							
VIBRATO (TYPES)							
DAILY DOSE (VITAMINS, MINERALS, AND HERBS)							

NOTES:

SONGS:

DAILY PRACTICE GUIDE

	MONDAY	TUESDAY	WEDNESDAY	THURSDAY	FRIDAY	SATURDAY	SUNDAY
VOCAL STRESS RELEASE							
FALSETTO SLIDE							
TRANSCENDING TONE							
THE SIREN							
THE BULLFROG							
VIBRATO (TYPES)							
DAILY DOSE (VITAMINS, MINERALS, AND HERBS)							

NOTES:

SONGS:

180

DAILY PRACTICE GUIDE

	MONDAY	TUESDAY	WEDNESDAY	THURSDAY	FRIDAY	SATURDAY	SUNDAY
VOCAL STRESS RELEASE							
FALSETTO SLIDE							
TRANSCENDING TONE							
THE SIREN							
THE BULLFROG							
VIBRATO (TYPES)							
DAILY DOSE (VITAMINS, MINERALS, AND HERBS)							

NOTES:

SONGS:

DAILY PRACTICE GUIDE

	MONDAY	TUESDAY	WEDNESDAY	THURSDAY	FRIDAY	SATURDAY	SUNDAY
VOCAL STRESS RELEASE							
FALSETTO SLIDE							
TRANSCENDING TONE							
THE SIREN							
THE BULLFROG							
VIBRATO (TYPES)							
DAILY DOSE (VITAMINS, MINERALS, AND HERBS)							

NOTES:

SONGS:

DAILY PRACTICE GUIDE

	MONDAY	TUESDAY	WEDNESDAY	THURSDAY	FRIDAY	SATURDAY	SUNDAY
VOCAL STRESS RELEASE							
FALSETTO SLIDE							
TRANSCENDING TONE							
THE SIREN							
THE BULLFROG							
VIBRATO (TYPES)							
DAILY DOSE (VITAMINS, MINERALS, AND HERBS)							

NOTES:

SONGS:

Printed in the United States
58310LVS00005B/21